Gateshead's Grand Houses

REDHEUGH HOUSE.

Sandra Brack
Gateshead Local History Society

Foreword

Gateshead Local History Society are due a huge vote of thanks for their sterling efforts in researching the history of Gateshead's large houses – many of which, sadly, are no longer with us. Who today can remember the glories of Redheugh Hall, South Dene Tower and the other equally grand houses which once existed here? Although some of the names live on in area and street names, the stories of the people who built and occupied them has, in many cases, been lost or buried in the pages of history.

This book reminds us of what Gateshead's lost houses looked like and tells the story of the people who owned them. And for those houses which remain, this is a chance to truly appreciate their importance.

This book deserves to be read – I hope you enjoy it and appreciate the hard work and research which has been carried out in order to produce it.

Anthea Lang
Former Local History and Heritage Manager, Gateshead Council

A tennis party at Orchard House in 1884. (See page 52.)

Previous page: *Redheugh Hall. (See page 10.)*

Copyright © Gateshead Local History Society 2012

First published in 2012 by

Summerhill Books
PO Box 1210, Newcastle-upon-Tyne NE99 4AH

www.summerhillbooks.co.uk

email: summerhillbooks@yahoo.co.uk

ISBN: 978-1-906721-53-4

Introduction

Gateshead has always lived within the shadow of its larger neighbour Newcastle and has struggled on occasions to keep its own identity. Whilst initiatives such as NewcastleGateshead are welcome joint ventures, Gateshead itself has a lot to offer and be proud of both today and from the past. Today we have The BALTIC and Sage along the regenerated Quayside area, forthcoming shopping, leisure and housing complex in the town centre, excellent leisure facilities, City of Sport; and award winning Saltwell Park. We also have some wonderful heritage.

Gateshead was made up of large estates which in time were divided into smaller areas upon which were built a number of houses, halls, villas and mansions, mostly owned by very wealthy and prosperous engineers, chemists, ship owners, mine owners, and men of industry.

Members of Gateshead Local History Society have compiled this book to share some of these lovely stately halls, houses, villas and mansions of Gateshead. It is by no means a comprehensive list, there are still many more buildings that have either gone now or are private residences tucked away behind high stone walls.

The book is split into ten sections starting at the River Tyne and moving across the town towards Wrekenton and remains roughly within the old Gateshead boundary of pre 1974. Each section ends with an Ordnance Survey map of 2012 showing the position of the house with a small black square or large black dot, the small black square indicates that the house is no longer there and the large black dot indicates that the house is still there today. By looking at the number of houses it is possible to get a flavour of how Gateshead looked and how important it was as a town in the 18th and 19th centuries.

We hope you enjoy our collection.

Sandra Brack
Secretary of Gateshead Local History Society

The fountain at the back of Whinney House. (See page 55.)

Acknowledgments

Without the generous help provided by Gateshead Council, the production of this book would not have been possible.

A great number of people have contributed to this book, of which we are very grateful. In particular we would like to thank:

Gateshead Local Studies, Gateshead Local History Society, Margaret Hall, Bob Dixon, Ian Daley, Alex Grant, Gordon Hudson, and special thanks to Mary Richardson for maps and Anthea Lang for support and foreword.

Where ever possible we have tried to contact the owner/occupiers of the houses we have taken photographs of to gain permission to use the image. We would like to thank the owner/occupiers of the following houses who have kindly allowed us permission to use a photograph of their property:

Aldersyde, Barrington Villa, Beaconside (St Peter's Presbytery), Bensham Grove, Chowdene Cottage, Clarendon House, Cotfield House, Craigielea, Denewell House, Eslington Villa, Fell Cottage, Fountains House, Glenbrooke, Granville House, Grove House, Hawksbury House, Hillcroft Lodge, Lindum House, New Biggin Villa, Novar House, Orchard House, Saltwell Dene East, Saltwell Dene West, Sheriff Mount North, Sheriff Mount South, The Chesters, The Crossways, The Dene, The Great House, The Grove, Villa (Old Dispensary), Westmorland House, Wood Dalling House, Woodside and Ythan Villa.

Please respect the privacy of the owners/occupiers of the houses included in this book.

Thanks also to Beamish Museum Archives for image of the Dance family; Andrew Bowker for image of Deckham Hall and Miles Bowker; Jennifer D Goddard for image of Carr Hill House and Peirson family; Mike Scott for image of The Great House; Mark Smiles for image of North Dene; David Thompson for image of Wishaw House; owners of Appleby House for painting of Appleby House and image of tennis party at Orchard House; and residents of Denewell House for painting of house by Gordon T Kell.

Also to all those photographers who had the foresight to take photographs of Gateshead so that we and future generations are able to see our past and how it has influenced what we see today.

All colour images copyright of Sandra Brack unless otherwise stated.

Whilst every effort has been made to contact and acknowledge due copyright within this book, we would like to thank those copyright holders of any material contained within this publication where this has not been possible.

Supported by

Section One

The houses and halls covered in this area are bordered between the River Tyne on the north, along Coatsworth Road, across to Saltwell View, down to Saltwell Road then heading north to the River Tyne.

Barrington Villa

Barrington Villa is shown on the Ordnance Survey map c1856-65, and is situated on Barrington Place off Bensham Road. The Villa is a narrow L shaped house one room deep, and appears to be two houses added together. It is thought that the building on the right is of older date which was a scullery with stairs to the upper floor, possibly servants' accommodation.

The building is of light brown brick, with a shallow hipped roof. From the front elevation the door is in the centre with a long window at each side of equal proportions, and three similar windows on the first level, all windows have stone lintels and sills, the doorway also has a stone lintel and frame.

Photograph taken – January 2011.

The house has a small garden to the front and side which is surrounded by a high stone wall, the garden at one time occupied the land along to Bensham Road. The surrounding wall was rebuilt closer to the house by Gateshead Council to allow for a footpath on Barrington Place.

The photograph left shows the curved staircase at Barrington Villa. The first occupant was Joseph Hume, a post office clerk, in 1856. Elizabeth Hawks widow of George Hawks also lived at Barrington Villa around 1865 and was also shown living there on the 1871 census. Around 1879 to 1886 James Hudson Scaife, a ship broker, lived there.

Photograph taken – July 2011.

Bensham Grove

Bensham Grove is situated on Sidney Grove, off Bensham Road. The house was owned by Joshua Watson in the early 1800s. Joshua Watson was a Quaker and cheesemonger who had lived over his shop in Newcastle. His son Joseph and grandson Robert Spence Watson enlarged the house which resulted in a mix of Georgian and Victorian features.

Artists, craftsmen, educationalists, reformers, poets and politicians have all been visitors of Robert and his wife Elizabeth at Bensham Grove. William Morris & Co were commissioned to redecorate in 1875 and installed fireplaces, tiles and carvings in addition to some notable stained glass windows. One such window shown below depicts Admiral Collingwood. The west side of the house looks out over the Tyne Valley and has a bay window and sun room.

After the death of Elizabeth Spence Watson in 1919 Bensham Grove became an Educational Settlement doing much work during the depression in the 1930s. In 1947, it was taken over by Gateshead Education Authority. Bensham Grove has been a Grade II listed building since 13th January 1983, it remains a centre for Adult Learning and a Community Centre, and still has many of the original features. In April 2012 it was awarded a Heritage Lottery Fund of £289,400 towards its restoration.

Courtesy of Gateshead Council (Local History Library Collection).

Photograph taken – June 2010.

Bensham Hall

Bensham Hall was built in the late 1840s; the Ordnance Survey Map of 1858 shows the position of Bensham Hall up from Saltwell Road about where Dunsmuir Grove is today. It was occupied by Edmund Crawshay, the ironmaster, from around 1850 for over 40

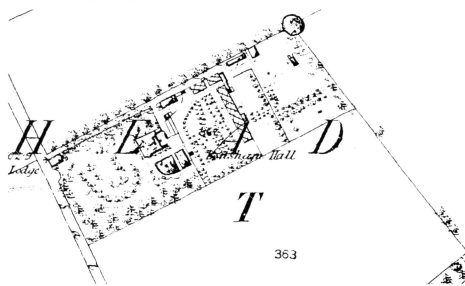

years. Edmund Crawshay was born in London, the son of George Crawshay, iron merchant, and the grandson of William Crawshay the 'Iron King' of South Wales. His mother was Josephe Louise Dufaud whose family owned the largest ironworks in France, at Fourchambault.

Edmund and his older brother George Crawshay took over the management of the Hawks, Stanley & Co. ironworks at

Gateshead, and by the mid-1840s the factory had become the largest ironworks on Tyneside, employing over a thousand workers. The company produced a vast range of iron goods, many of which were exported to India and the Far East. In 1889 the 'New Greenwich' ironworks of Hawks, Crawshay & Sons at Gateshead suddenly closed as they were unable to compete with Armstrong at Elswick. Crawshay was Mayor of Gateshead in 1865 and became a member of the North of England Institute of Mining and Mechanical Engineers on the 4th December 1869.

The house and grounds were acquired by John Ross in 1894 for building. The streets Stirling Terrace, Saltwell Road, Dunsmuir Grove and Kelvin Grove were all built on the grounds of Bensham Hall. The Stirling public house was originally built as a house for John Ross before becoming a public house.

Bensham Low House

Bensham Low House was situated on Lobley Hill Road, down from Victoria Road; roughly where Armstrong House Care Home is today. Some residents were around 1870 to 1871 Mr R Rutherford, a cart proprietor, Mr W Scott, a brick manufacturer and Mr W

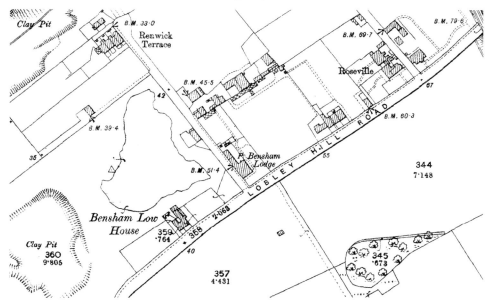

Fearn, a brick maker. Mr C Barries, the Danish Consul, lived at Bensham Low House around 1873 to 1877 and around 1893 Mr W Hindson, a manager. The footprint of Bensham Low House was slightly smaller than Bensham Grove.

Bensham Tower

Bensham Tower was up from Saltwell Road close to Saltwell Place, and was built in 1853 for Charles John Pearson. The house was built in the gothic style and had a small lake within landscaped grounds, the footprint was slightly smaller than Bensham Grove. Pearson was a builder with premises at 194 High Street, Gateshead.

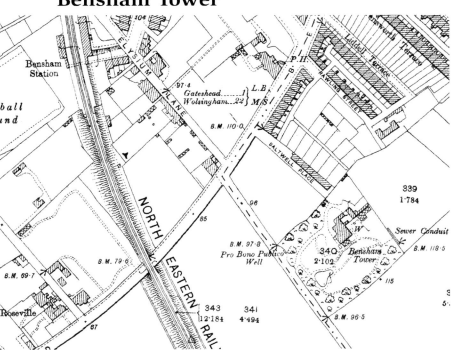

A later resident was William Galloway, a nail manufacturer, who lived there until 1890. Galloway's premises, established in the late 1850s were located at the end of Sunderland Road, and although the firm only employed about 25 to 50 people by 1900, it was able to take business from the giants of Hawks and Abbot.

The company also held an agency for French and American steam cars. In 1952 the company moved to Blaydon having been taken over by the industrial giant Guest, Keen and Nettlefold (GKN) in 1965. Bensham Tower was demolished around 1895.

Cotfield House

Cotfield House is on Bensham Road opposite St Cuthbert's Church and was built in 1806 for Thomas Thompson, a prosperous timber and raff merchant with offices in Broad Chare, Newcastle. A raff merchant is a dealer in lumber and odd refuse. Thompson was also a local song writer, known most notably for the New Keel Row and Canny Newcastle. He died while trying to protect his property on the river during a flood on 9th January 1816, aged 43.

Courtesy of Gateshead Council (Local History Library Collection).

Photograph taken – 5th June 2010.

Other occupants of Cotfield House have been Edward and Mary Graham who were both buried in St Edmund's graveyard, Mary died 15th August 1846 aged 56 years and Edmund died 14th March 1868 aged 77 years. Around 1870 to 1875 William Muschamp, a paper manufacturer, lived at Cotfield. Muschamp was elected a member of the Natural History Society of Northumberland, Durham and Newcastle upon Tyne in 1870 and was Mayor of Gateshead in 1872.

The 1901 census lists Dr Alfred Cox living at Cotfield House. His surgery entrance was the lower door on Bensham Road, to the left inside was the dispensary and on the right was the waiting room with wooden benches around the walls. Dr Cox OBE was a GP, surgeon and JP. He was co-founder of the Queen Victoria Nursing Association. He was Medical Secretary to the BMA, 1912-31, and was awarded the Gold Medal of the BMA in 1931. Dr Cox also lived at Westview House just east of Cotfield where a blue plaque was unveiled in March 2011 to commemorate his work.

Cotfield House is now divided into two properties and privately owned.

Field House

Field House is referred to as Enfield House on the Ordnance Survey map c1856-65 just off Enfield House Lane (now Saltwell View). On the c1894-99 Ordnance Survey map the house is called Field House and Saltwell View is called Field House Road.

John Dobson had designed the house in 1813 which was one of his earliest commissions. In the 1830s Field House was occupied by Joseph Shield, a Newcastle coal-fitter and ship owner, and by 1838 the estate contained a vinery and was described as having a sloping lawn with an extensive view of Ravensworth.

In the 1880s Field House was occupied by Arthur Newall; and the 1891 census shows John George Sowerby, aged 41, a glass manufacturer, his wife Amy Margaret, six children and four servants who had previously lived at Ravenshill, living at Field House. Their older son John Lawrence was listed as a 'glass house manager', who stayed with the firm for only

five years before he left, and in 1912 emigrated to Canada. The house was let as a private boys' school in 1895 and the 1911 census shows Mr T Errington, a cart proprietor, living there. Field House was demolished in 1931.

Hill Field House

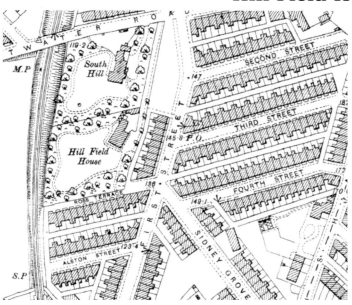

Hill Field House was situated behind First Street, Bensham. A resident around 1893 was Mr Alfred S Palmer, a mining engineer. He was born in 1835 and from 1853-54 he was a member of the North of England Institute of Mining and Mechanical Engineers. In 1855 he was a viewer at Seaton Burn. In 1893 he was Chairman of Heworth School Board and Colliery Agent at Dunston. In 1894 he was agent to John Bowes and Partners at Dunston Colliery.

Ravensworth Villa

Ravensworth Villa was situated at the north end of Hill Field Street and shown on the Ordnance Survey map c1856-65 but is not named on the Ordnance Survey map c1894-99. The villa was near Sedgewick Villa, Barrington Villa and Claremount House. Thomas Crashwaite Angus, a hide merchant, was a resident around June 1859.

Redheugh Hall

The Redheugh Estate was established in the 13th century by the Redheugh family. During the reign of Henry VI it came into the possession of the Whites. Sir Francis Liddell bought the estate in about 1620 from Robert White and his descendants conveyed it to the Earl of Derwentwater. Redheugh Hall was built in the late 17th century. Between 1713 and 1748 the estate was occupied by Lady Mary Radcliff who sold it to Dr Adam Askew who bought it for his son Henry. The Askew family held the estate until the 1870s. The house originally had five bays and was enlarged by the Askews who added North and South wings. Several acres of ornamental grounds and plantations surrounded the house.

The mansion was leased to William Cuthbert, the Newcastle glass manufacturer in 1835. George Hawks (pictured below) the leading partner in Hawks, Crawshay and sons also lived at Redheugh Hall. George Hawks was Gateshead's first Mayor in 1836 and was subsequently re-elected twice more in 1848 and 1849; he also became Deputy Lieutenant of County Durham. Hawks did not pay great attention to his mayoral duties due to his many other engagements although he was very fond of civic honours and mixing with dignitaries. However he also adopted a paternalistic and caring attitude towards his employees having built housing for some of his workforce. His company was also noted for the building of the High Level Bridge in 1849.

REDHEUGH HOUSE.

Courtesy of Gateshead Council (Local History Library Collection).

His death on 3rd October 1863 was greeted with great dismay and widely reported in local newspapers. He was buried in the family vault at St Cuthbert's, Gateshead. A memorial statue was unveiled in October 1865 on Windmill Hills Park, and although re located the statue still stands there today.

The construction of the Newcastle and Carlisle railway passed through the estate near to the house, and the opening of the Redheugh Bridge in 1871 affected the development and Redheugh Hall could no longer be described as a 'gentleman's seat'. In 1912 it was a store house, a bad fire in 1920 left it roofless, and it steadily decayed until demolished in 1935/36.

Courtesy of Gateshead Council (Local History Library Collection).

Roseville

Roseville was situated near Bensham Road between Bensham Lodge and the railway line about where Kyle Road is today. Roseville must have been divided into separate premises. One resident around 1870 was Gibson Kyle, an architect, who lived there for more than thirty years. Around 1879 Mr G Charlton, a JP, and Miss I Murray also lived at Roseville. Other residents have been around 1887 Mr G C Bowman, a warehouseman; in 1889 Mr E Borlase, a clerk; and around 1897 Mr G Mitcheson, a hardware man; and Thomas Martin Conradi, a vice-consul. The 1901 census shows Roseville being occupied by William Donnelly, a property owner, and William Thomas Dance, a merchant.

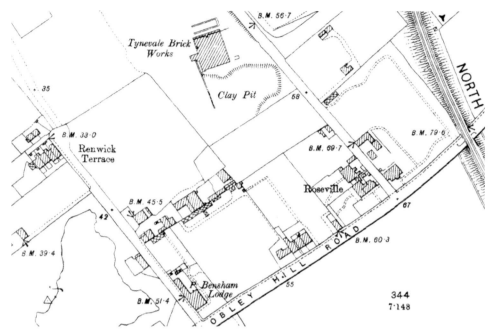

Sedgewick Villa

Sedgewick Villa is shown on the Ordnance Survey map c1856-65, but is not named on the Ordnance Survey map c1894-99. The Villa was situated near the north end of Coatsworth Road opposite to where Affleck Street is today. One resident was Frederick Clark, a draper, the son of William Clark of Doncaster and his wife Phebe, daughter of the late George Goundary of Newcastle who had married on 19th March 1851. Frederick Clark was on the committee of the Mechanics Institute in 1854. On 5th February 1864 at Sedgewick Villa, Phebe gave birth to a daughter who was named Phebe Fiona.

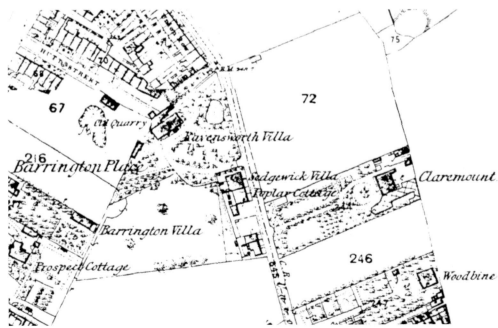

South Hill

South Hill was situated off Derwentwater Road near to Hill Field House. The grounds were lawned and surrounded by trees with the entrance on Derwentwater Road. One resident around 1873 to 1893 was William Spencer, a rope manufacturer. Spencer worked at Dixon, Corbitt Ltd.

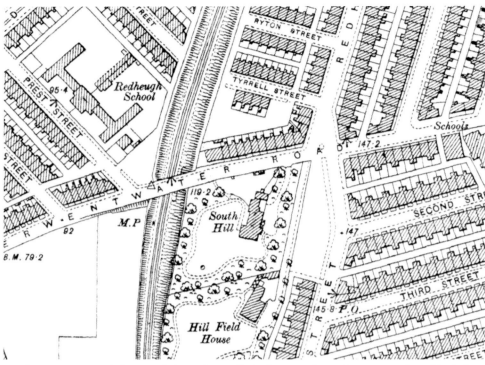

Tynevale House

Tynevale House was situated on Derwentwater Road; planning permission was approved in 1864 for George Dixon who lived there for more than twenty years. Dixon was a rope manufacturer of Dixon, Corbitt Ltd who later merged with R S Newall and Co. Both companies established at the Teams in 1840. Dixon, Corbitt Ltd was on the east bank and R S Newall on the west bank, and had worked together for many years before amalgamation in 1887. One of their famous exploits concerned Cleopatra's Needle. Newall's supplied the wire rope and Dixon, Corbitt the steel caisson which were used to tow the obelisk to London from Egypt by sea. The amalgamated concern was taken over by the Willington Haggie firm and in 1959 became part of the British Ropes Group. The 1881 census shows George Dixon's son, George R T Dixon, aged 24, living at Tynevale. He was a sanitary ware merchant with premises at No 1 Wellington Street, Gateshead.

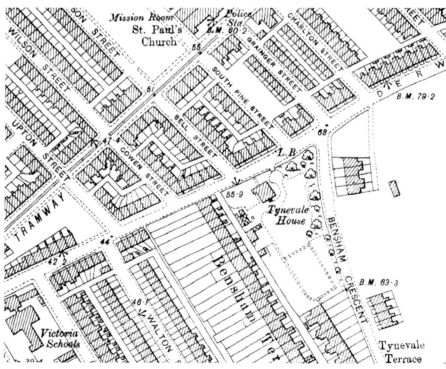

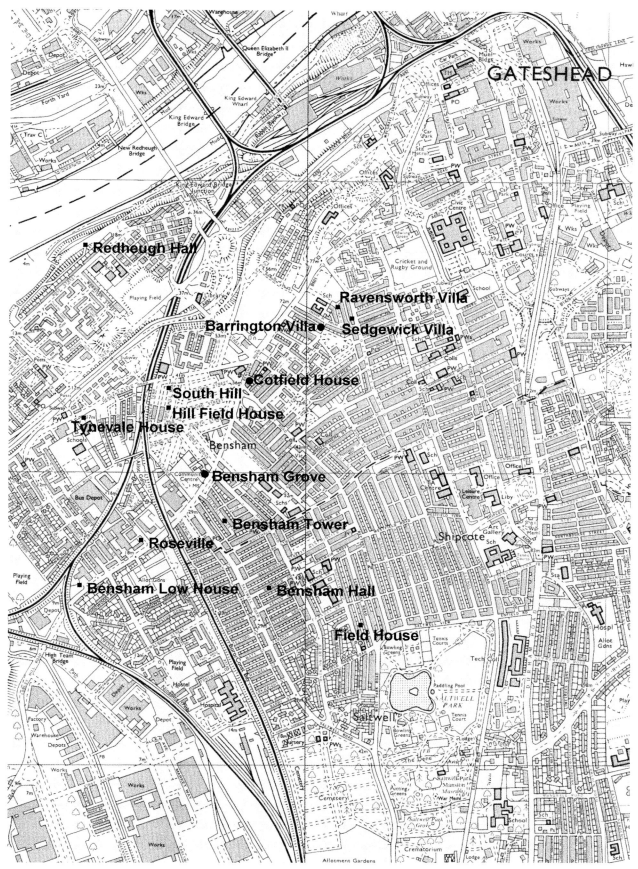

Key: Small black square ■ indicates the house is no longer there.

Large black circle ● indicates the house is still there.

Contains Ordnance Survey data © Crown copyright and database right 2012.

Section Two

The houses and halls covered in this area are located south of the River Tyne, up Askew Road, across to Bensham Bank, along Coatsworth Road to Whitehall Road, then east to Cramer Street, across to Sunderland Road and back to the River Tyne.

Back Field House

Back Field House was recorded on John Bell's land survey map of 1835. The Ordnance Survey map right shows the house was situated on Park Lane. The house is near the railway line to the east and north and close to nurseries to the west. One resident was Joseph Stoker, a farmer, around 1859.

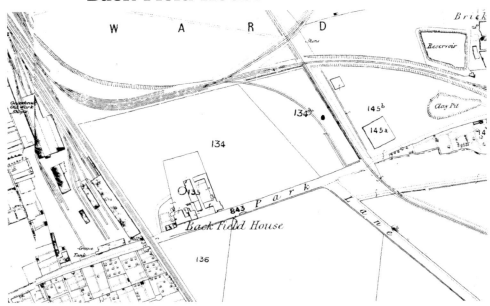

© Crown copyright and Landmark Information Group Ltd. All rights reserved 2012.

Bedford House

Bedford House was number 84 Bensham Road, near the Borough Arms, Gateshead. The house was built of smooth stone to the front; it had a small front garden which led up to railed steps to a distinctive stone porch. This picture was taken in July 1971 possibly just before demolition, as one upstairs window is boarded and a number of windows are broken. Some occupants have been around 1874 Mr J Barrett, a tobacconist, in 1889 Mr W White, a surgeon, in 1893 Mr W W Grey a surgeon, and around 1897 a Mrs M F Wilson.

Courtesy of Gateshead Council (Local History Library Collection).

Claremount House

Claremount House is shown on the Ordnance Survey map c1856-65, but is not named on the Ordnance Survey map c1894-99. The house was situated between where Claremont North Avenue and Claremont South Avenue are today. The map shows the entrance was on Union Lane, now Coatsworth Road, with a long drive up to the house. A number of streets have been built close by and the Union Workhouse can be seen to the south.

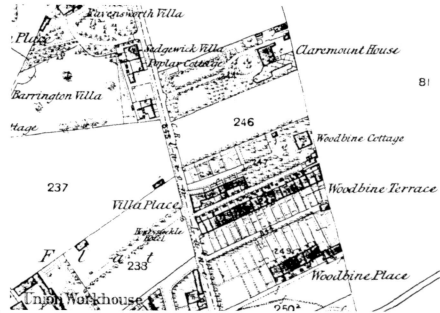

Two residents of Claremount House were David and Peter Haggie of Haggie Brothers around 1853 to 1856. Haggie brothers were rope and chain manufacturers and timber merchants on South Shore. Their brother, Robert Hood Haggie, set up his own rope making business in Willington employing a number of women who famously were known as 'Haggies Angels'.

David Haggie was Mayor of Gateshead in 1853 – Courtesy of Gateshead Council (Local History Library Collection).

Cramer Dyke House (or Camer Dyke)

Cramer Dyke used to be a great pit, which had been worked from earliest times, and is sometimes referred to as Camer Dyke. The house is shown on John Bell's land survey map of 1835, and stood on the opposite side to Cross Street, Old Durham Road, near to where Cramer Street is today.

One notable resident was William Falla II (1761-1830) who owned one of several local nurseries. The business was established in Hebburn by his father William Falla (1739-1804) which he later moved to Felling. The catalogue in 1827 offered no fewer than 415 varieties of fruit trees. William Falla II was a founder member of the Botanical and Horticultural

Society of Durham, Northumberland and Newcastle upon Tyne. He carried out the first systematic plantation of trees around St Mary's Church, Heworth, in 1823.

William Falla II died on the 4th August 1830 in his 70th year and was buried at St Mary's Church, Heworth. Sadly William Falla III (1799-1836) was no match for his father's acumen and committed suicide in Ravensworth Woods, when unable to satisfy his creditors.

Other residents at Cramer Dyke House have been around 1858 to 1877 Mr W Scott, a builder, and in 1879 Mr T H Burnett, a chemical manufacturer.

Gateshead House

In 1595 William Riddell Esq, Mayor of Newcastle, erected a large mansion called Gateshead House which stood behind the old Hospital of St Edmund's on the High Street.

Several generations of the Riddell's lived at Gateshead House. Sir Peter received his Knighthood from King James I in May 1617. During the siege of Newcastle in 1644 Sir T Riddell occupied the house when it was much damaged by the Scots troopers. Later the house and grounds passed into the hands of the Claverings.

Courtesy of Gateshead Council (Local History Library Collection).

The picture above shows Gateshead House in ruins, caused by a riotous mob on 27th January 1746. The Duke of Cumberland and King George's army were moving north to

meet Bonnie Prince Charlie and his Scottish followers; the route would take them through Gateshead near Gateshead House. As news came that the army was crossing Gateshead Fell the crowd that had gathered became excited and in order to get a good view some climbed on the walls of Gateshead House. The gardener was not happy and chased the crowd who turned angry. They broke into Gateshead House, set the place on fire and looted many of the priceless heirlooms.

The gateway to Gateshead House pictured left was moved to the left side of St Edmund's and at one time stood between St Edmund's and Ellison School. When Holy Trinity was built to the left of St Edmund's the gateway was moved to the forecourt of St Edmund's Chapel where it stands today.

Courtesy of Gateshead Council.

Granville House

Granville House is situated on the corner of Granville Street and Durham Road next to the Durham Road Baptist Church. The house built in brick has two storeys with attic rooms, the windows and door all have stone lintels, and two bay windows can still be seen.

Some occupiers have been Mr J Todd (MD), a surgeon, in 1897 and around 1918 London Joint Stock Bank Ltd. In 1935 Granville House became the Midland Bank Ltd; the house is currently occupied by a loans company.

Photograph taken – 5th June 2010.

Greenesfield House

An earlier house named Greenesfield House was located near to where Hudson Street is today, and was a three storey property. Councillor Edmund Graham sold the house and estate to the Brandling Junction Railway Co. Later falling into financial difficulties the company sold the Greenesfield estate to a builder, Councillor Charles J. Pearson who sold the house with part of the land to Councillor Thomas Cummins for £1,150.

The house and land was then sold to the Corporation for £1,300 and was converted into a Town Hall. Councillor Cummins was the first Mayor to preside in the new building.

The building was also used as a Borough Magistrates Court, Police Station and from 1847 the County Court. Greenesfield House continued as the Town Hall until May 1866; the Council had received notice that the house was in the way of the projected Team Valley Railway Line, which forms part of the direct route through Gateshead to London. The new line was built between 1865

Courtesy of Gateshead Council (Local History Library Collection).

and 1867, the Town Hall was demolished in 1867 and Gateshead West station was built on the site.

The second house named Greenesfield (pictured above) was near the site of Barns Close; one known occupant around 1893 was Wilson Worsdell the Locomotive Superintendant for the North Eastern Railway from 1890 to 1910. Wilson Worsdell was born 7th September 1850, the 10th child (4th son) of Nathanial and Mary and was brought up in the Quaker faith. He was the younger brother of T W Worsdell and grandson of the coach builder Thomas Clarke Worsdell.

Wilson Worsdell was appointed Assistant Locomotive Superintendent of the NER in 1883 and became Locomotive Superintendent in 1890. This title was renamed to Chief Mechanical Engineer in 1902. After a visit of senior NER staff to the USA, Worsdell chose boilers of diameter 5ft 6in for many of his locomotive classes. One of the most powerful locomotives in Britain at that time was his 4-4-2 Atlantic (LNER C6) design, and he was the first to introduce a passenger 4-6-0 locomotive to Britain. Worsdell died in 1920. Greenesfield House was also at one time used as Gateshead Clinic.

Holly House

Holly House, one of the town's oldest buildings was situated on the north east of the Windmill Hills. Reputed to have been built in the 17th century, it was altered in the late 18th century. Holly House was a private house until the beginning of the 20th century when it was bought by the Corporation and used by the Welfare and Social Services Department.

Some occupiers have been Mr Henry Clapham, a ship broker and Mr E Turnbull, a gentleman, around 1870. Henry Clapham in 1870 was elected a member of the Natural History Society of Northumberland, Durham and Newcastle upon Tyne. In 1873 Mr T Armstrong, referred to as a 'gentleman', also lived at Holly House. It was abandoned in 1971 and stood vandalised and derelict, there was a campaign to preserve the house but it was demolished.

Courtesy of Gateshead Council (Local History Library Collection).

Park House

The Park estate was the Bishop of Durham's park in Gateshead, until the 17th century when it was leased to the Lord of the Manor. In 1716 William Cotesworth became Lord of the Manor.

Park House was rebuilt in 1723 and then enlarged between 1729 and 1733 by Cotesworth's son-in-law Henry Ellison. James Gibbs supervised the design. The house was brick with stone dressings, and was surrounded by a small landscaped enclosure, with lawns, trees, and a fish pond. It was approached from an entrance lodge on Sunderland Road slightly to the east of John Street.

Courtesy of Gateshead Council (Local History Library Collection).

The Ellisons kept Park House until 1825, it was then leased to a number of local industrialists, the Cookson's, Charles Bulmer, and Alexander Grey of Friars Goose Chemical Works; and Henry and Alfred Allhusen. The 1881 census shows Alfred Allhusen, aged 27, his wife Fanny, seven children, his mother and servants all lived there.

In 1884 the house was acquired by Clarke Chapman and converted into offices. In November 1891 it was gutted by a severe fire and was reconstructed internally standing within Clarke Chapman-John Thompson Works. Park House was demolished after Clarke Chapman closed; the land is now a housing estate.

It was thought that Park House was the house referred to as Gateshead Hall in Charlotte Bronte's novel Jane Eyre, hence the streets around the area were named after the Bronte family and their novels. Even though this was subsequently disproved, the street names remained.

Romulus House

Romulus House is shown on the Ordnance Survey map c1856-65 and was situated off Bensham Bank near Windmill Hills. The house was sold up and demolished in 1866 and James Street built on its site from 1868.

Villa

Courtesy of Newcastle City Library.

The Villa is situated on the corner of West Street and Nelson Street and was originally designed as a private house, probably in the 1830s.

The Villa has two storeys of red brick with Georgian sash windows and a stone pillared entrance. The picture left shows a metal railing surrounded the house at one time. The 1851 census shows Joseph Willis Swinburne, aged 24, living at the Villa with his mother, older sister, four younger sisters, two younger brothers and two servants.

In 1855 Gateshead Corporation bought the villa to house the dispensary. It remained a dispensary until the National Health Service began in 1947 and was for many years' council offices; it is now occupied by a travel company.

Photograph taken – 11th June 2010.

Woodbine Villa

Woodbine Villa is situated at the top of Villa Place, off Coatsworth Road. The villa has two storeys and attic rooms; the front is of smooth stone, the sides being more rough stone.

The property was quite a substantial plot as can be noted from a For Sale advert: 'To be sold or let by private contract, Woodbine Villa, with a coach house, stable, and about an acre of garden ground in front, with a good supply of water.' (Gateshead Observer, 1st March 1845)

Occupants in the 1870s have included Thomas Dodds, a commercial merchant, his wife, nine children and two servants. The owner in 1899 was Mr A McIntyre who was granted planning approval on 4th January for the conversion of Woodbine Villa into tenement property.

In 1911 the Villa was split into four apartments; occupants were Mr I Harte, a decorator; Mrs E Horn, a dressmaker; H Birtley and Mr J Summers, a joiner. Woodbine Villa is now split into six apartments.

Photograph taken – 31st August 2011.

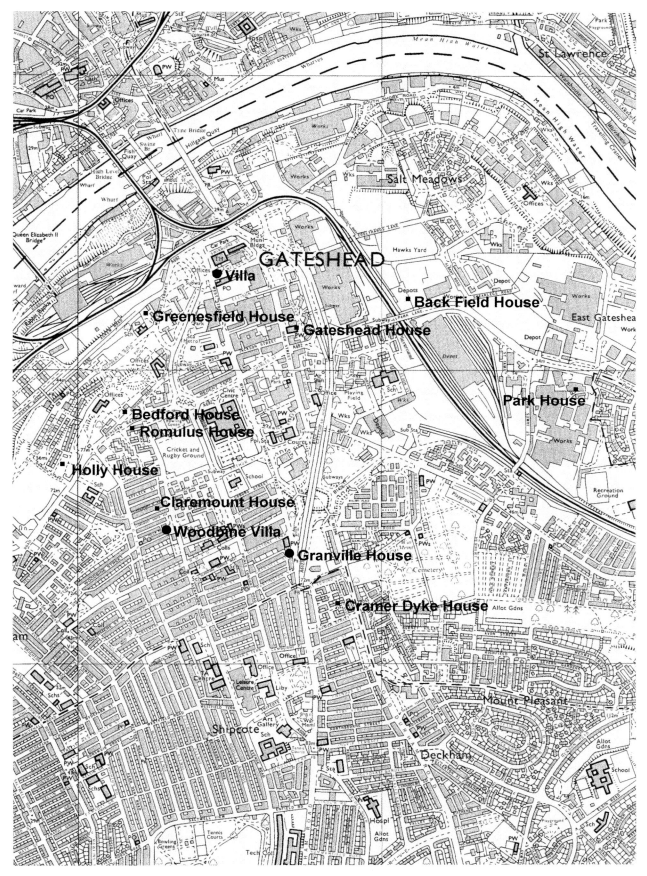

Key: Small black square ■ indicates the house is no longer there.

Large black circle ● indicates the house is still there.

Contains Ordnance Survey data © Crown copyright and database right 2012.

Section Three

The houses and halls covered in this area are located between Avenue Road and Durham Road and from Camborne Grove to the bottom of Valley Drive.

Bloomfield

On the Ordnance Survey map c1856-65 this house is called Walker Villa, and on the Ordnance Survey map c1894-99 it was called Bloomfield. Bloomfield was quite a large sixteen roomed house which stood in its own grounds on Durham Road between Park View to North Dene. The picture right, taken from a postcard, shows Bloomfield from Saltwell Park, its position can be seen high above the Pavilion on the Promenade.

Courtesy of Gateshead Council (Local History Library Collection).

In 1850 the estate was occupied by Thomas Robson, who was described as a Farm and Horse Dealer. On the 30th August 1859 the property was sold to Michael Green, a merchant, who died on 7th May 1868 aged 54 and is buried in Gateshead East Cemetery. The house was then left to his wife Mary, who lived there until her death on 5th December 1889.

On 19th May 1890 the house was conveyed to Robert Affleck who is described as "of Gateshead, gentleman". Robert Affleck lived at Bloomfield with his wife Georgina, four sons, two daughters and four servants. Robert was a Justice of the Peace and Alderman, a house agent and property owner and Chairman of the Board of Guardians of Gateshead.

The portrait left is of Robert Affleck who died on the 3rd August 1910, following a burst appendix. The 1911 census shows Georgina Affleck, aged 57 of Fatfield, her married daughter, son-in-law, grandchildren and two servants living at Bloomfield. On the 3rd February 1912 the property was sold to Hastings Russell Eastcott, an engineer, who lived here until his death on 21st June 1935, after which the property was sold to Gateshead Corporation. He was the son of Harry Eastcott of Endsleigh. After the Second World War the house was used as Council Offices of the Borough Treasurer, and was later absorbed into Gateshead Technical College on Durham Road. Bloomfield House was demolished in 1957.

Courtesy of Gateshead Council (Local History Library Collection).

Dene House

Dene House is situated on a small drive between North Dene House and The Drive, off Durham Road, and was originally called Red House (shown on map right).

The house is of red brick with red roof tiles; the front which faces north has two storeys whilst the sides and back have three storeys, the west facing side has lovely bay windows looking out over the Team Valley. From 1901 Mr F Emley, a solicitor, lived at Red House and from around 1925 Mr John Adamson Greener a coal exporter lived there. In later years the house was known as Dowsett House and is now known as Dene House.

© Crown copyright and Landmark Information Group Ltd. All rights reserved 2012.

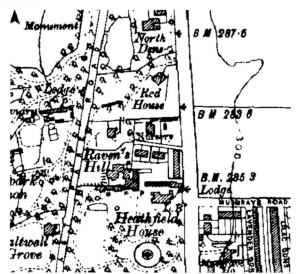

Enfield House

Enfield House was a nineteen roomed house and stood at the top right hand corner of Enfield Road and Durham Road, roughly where the former Gateshead College car park is today. William Wailes of Saltwell Towers, the stained glass manufacturer, originally owned the land which was conveyed on 23rd January 1865 to Thomas B Neilson of Gateshead, an auctioneer. Thomas Neilson received planning approval to build a villa on 4th August 1865. On the 28th January 1870 Thomas Neilson became bankrupt and on the 4th August 1870 the Mortgagees of the property was conveyed to Richard Mosley Stark of Newcastle a merchant.

On the 9th October 1872 Richard Mosley Stark died and his widow Mary Stark conveyed the property to John Walton Robinson of Gateshead. Robinson was a cheesemonger and provision merchant, the 1881 census shows John Walton Robinson, aged 63, lived at Enfield House with his wife Anne, sister in law, granddaughter and two servants.

Robinson sold Enfield House on the 1st May 1886 to Walter De Lancey Willson, a

Courtesy of Gateshead Council (Local History Library Collection).

grocer from Bishop Auckland. Willson started a grocery company in Bishop Auckland in 1875 with Stephen Aitchison; by 1950 they had 193 shops. Willson was Mayor of Gateshead in 1891 and 1892.

The 1901 census shows Willson, aged 55, living at Enfield House with his wife Mary, aged 47, three daughters and four servants. Walter Willson died on the 7th June 1907 and the property was conveyed to Gateshead Corporation on the 31st December 1920. At a later date the house was used as a girls training college before Gateshead Technical College was built.

Enfield Villa

Enfield Villa, comprising of nine rooms, is situated at the top of Enfield Road on Durham Road. Some residents have been in 1858 Mr C A Scarthmore, a commercial

traveller; and around 1870 Mr W W Carrick, a clerk. The 1891 census shows Hannah Carrick aged 52, three sons and servant, and the 1911 census shows a Lawrence Collier. Around 1918 to 1935 Mrs A L Tankerville, a professor of music, also lived at Enfield Villa. Enfield Villa is currently split into two apartments.

Courtesy of Gateshead Council (Local History Library Collection).

North Dene

North Dene was built for Richard Hodgson in 1853 where he resided until his death on 26th May 1885. North Dene has fifteen rooms and is built of stone with an impressive stone entrance porch to the main door; it is surrounded by gardens with a balustrade to the west looking out over Saltwell Park. Hodgson was a JP and Mayor of Gateshead in 1854 and 1871. He owned a grindstone quarry in Windy Nook and was a Director of the North East Banking Co. and also the Tyne Steam Shipping Co. He was a subscriber to the Historical Register of Remarkable Events, and a founder member of the local branch of the RSPCA and served as their president for a number of years.

Courtesy of Mark Smiles.

The photograph below is of Richard Wellington Hodgson (1812-1885).

Another resident was Joseph Thompson a coal owner, who gained planning approval on 4th May 1887 for a billiard room at North Dene; and in 1906, aged 61, he still resided there, a widower, with his daughter, niece and three servants. In 1914 Mr Harry Walker Eastcott, an engineer, lived at North Dene, and gained planning approval on 5th August for an Entrance Lodge on East Park Road at the South West corner of North Dene estate. He was the son of Harry Eastcott of Endsleigh. From September 1953 until the early 1960s the house was used as an annex to Gateshead Grammar School and was later used as part of Gateshead Technical College on Durham Road. North Dene now stands empty within the College grounds. The house is currently owned by Miller Homes with the intention to be converted into apartments.

Courtesy of Gateshead Council (Local History Library Collection).

Park View

On the 4th September 1877 the land was conveyed to Mr John Douglas of Gateshead, a corn merchant, and planning approval was granted on 6th February 1878 for a detached villa on Durham Road. Mr Douglas erected the house on this land between that date and 1879. Park View was a nine roomed house situated between Bloomfield and Enfield House. In 1870 Douglas was elected a member of the Natural History Society of Northumberland, Durham and Newcastle upon Tyne. John Douglas died on the 12th October 1880 and the property was sold. The 1891 census shows David Davies, aged 52, an iron manufacturer, his wife Elizabeth, aged 44, their son John William, aged 24, and young son David Sidney, aged 4. In 1900 after Elizabeth's death on 21st October the property subsequently devolved to her

Courtesy of Gateshead Council (Local History Library Collection).

son, David Sidney Davies. David Sidney Davies is described as an iron master and resided in the property until about the time of its sale to Gateshead Corporation on the 26th July 1950. Gateshead Technical College was built on the site and opened on 15th November 1955. The college closed in January 2008 and the site is soon to be Park View housing by Miller Homes.

Rodsley House

Rodsley House is shown on John Bell's land survey map of 1835 and was situated on Avenue Road near Shipcote Lane. The house had been occupied since 1853 by John Greene a grocer and oil merchant, who was a member of the Royal Agricultural Society of England. The 1881 census shows Charles Robinson Green, aged 35, an oil merchant, his wife Grace, aged 30, two sons, one daughter and six servants lived there with a coachman in the lodge. Rodsley House was demolished sometime before 1931.

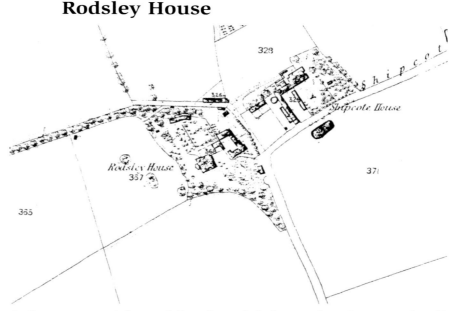

Shipcote House

The 1841 census shows that George Sowerby lived at Shipcote House. Sowerby was a colliery owner and member of the Sowerby family who had been manufacturing glass since 1760. Shipcote House was also the home of Thomas Rankin Strang around 1876, a glass-stainer, who was married to a daughter of William Wailes. Strang joined the business in 1861, when the firm became known as Wailes and Strang. The Chancel windows of St Helen's, Low Fell are by Wailes and Strang of Newcastle.

The 1881 census shows another resident of Shipcote House was John Pattinson, an analytical chemist, his wife Mary Jane, seven children and two servants; the family were still there in 1890. The house was later used as a Trade Union Club, but was demolished in September 1931. The old Shipcote baths occupies the site.

Courtesy of Gateshead Council (Local History Library Collection).

Shipcote Villa

Shipcote Villa was situated around the Durham Road and Camborne Place area not far from South Close Villa, and seems to have been spilt into apartments.

The 1871 census shows Mr Thomas William Dance (Major) JP, a corn merchant, his wife, three daughters, two sons, a nurse and three servants living at Shipcote Villa. The Dance family lived there for over thirty years. The 1871 census also shows Mr Edward Cully, a corn and flour merchant, his wife, four daughters and two servants living at Shipcote Villa. By 1883 Mr Henry Strachan, a ship broker, who had an office on the quayside, and his family were living at Shipcote Villa. The Strachan family lived there for many years. In 1893 Henry Strachan's part of Shipcote Villa was left to his wife Mrs S Strachan, and by 1897 it was left to their son Mr R Strachan. Mr R Strachan also a ship broker was Borough Magistrate in 1915. Other residents of Shipcote Villa were in 1894 Mr William Grey Pearson a manager, and from 1925 Mr D S Bowran an iron merchant.

The picture below shows members of the Dance family.

Courtesy of Beamish Museum Archives.

South Close Villa

South Close Villa was built for Edward Eccles who was granted planning approval on 4th April 1862. The Villa was situated on Durham Road just past Shipcote Lane. Edward Eccles was a colliery owner and lived at South Close Villa for at least thirty years. Other residents around 1918 to 1935 were the Misses Cameron. The grounds of South Close Villa are now a park area on Durham Road and Shipcote Lane.

Courtesy of Gateshead Council (Local History Library Collection).

Summerfield

Summerfield was built for William Henry Angus who was granted planning approval on 6th April 1870. The villa was situated on the Durham Turnpike, roughly opposite Lindum House, set back off Durham Road around where Silverdale Terrace stands today. The footprint of Summerfield was slightly smaller than that of Enfield House.

   William Henry Angus was a merchant, and lived at Summerfield for more than twenty years with his wife Anne and two servants. The 1901 census shows John Waugh, a brick manufacturer, his wife, six children and two servants living at Summerfield.

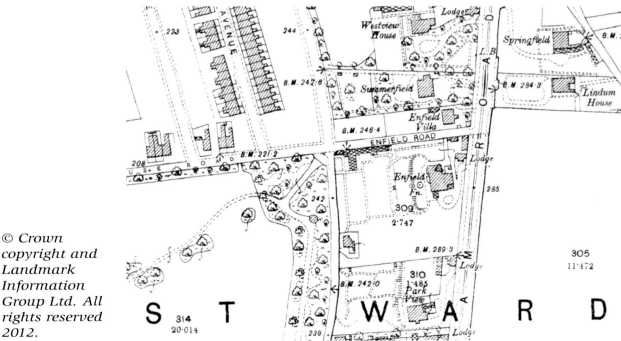

The Crossways

The Crossways is situated on the corner of Shipcote Lane and Durham Road. The house has two storeys with large attic rooms and a very unusual shaped roof. A resident in 1918 was Dr W J Durant a surgeon. The building later became premises for Group4 and is now The Yehoshua and Perry Tager Vocational Centre.

Photograph taken – June 2010.

Westview House

In 1872 Mr John Rowell had been given planning approval for a villa on Durham Road. Westview House was situated behind Durham Road, approximately where Silverdale and Patterdale Terrace are today, with a lodge on Durham Road. The footprint of Westview House was slightly smaller than that of Enfield House. The 1881 census shows Barbara Rowell, aged 70, a widow, daughter Dorothy and two servants living at Westview House. In 1918 Mr P E Carron a dentist; and around 1935 Mr N Lunn, a gentleman, lived at Westview.

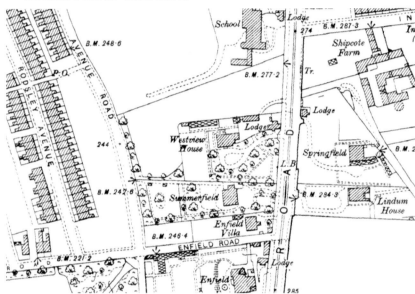

© Crown copyright and Landmark Information Group Ltd. All rights reserved 2012.

Wishaw House

Wishaw House was situated on Durham Road next to the park between Shipcote Lane and Camborne Place. One owner was Mr Thomas Russell Jarvie, a veterinary surgeon, who on 5th June 1907 gained planning approval for a new covered coach yard and to alter the position of the coach house. His wife Amy died in 1931 and Mr Jarvie resided at Wishaw House until 1935 at which time Mrs M Toward lived there. The house was also used as a Careers Office in the 1970s and 1980s and was later demolished. The Wishaw House petrol station was extended, and closed mid 2000s; the land is now New Forest Eco Friendly housing.

Courtesy of David Thompson 1986.

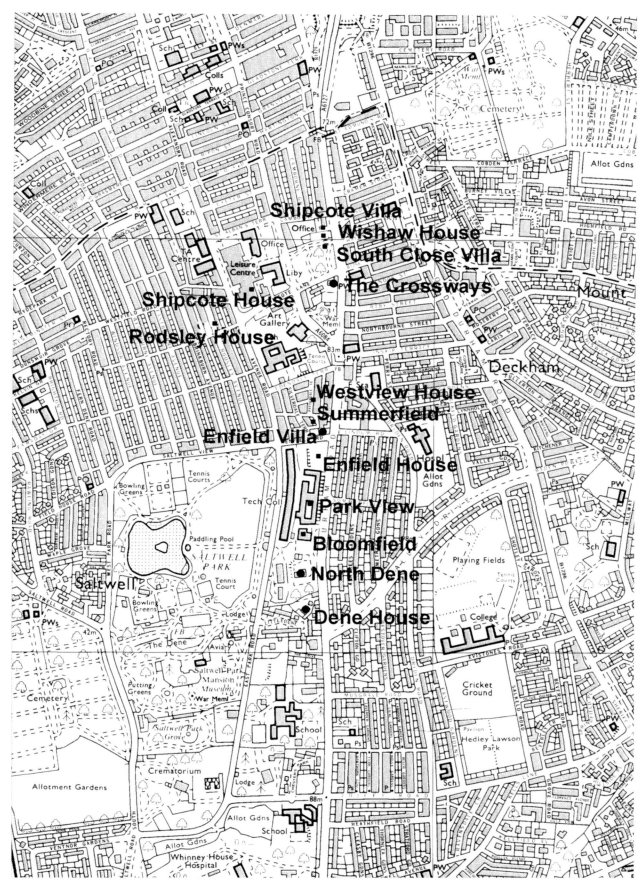

Key: Small black square   ■   indicates the house is no longer there.

   Large black circle   ●   indicates the house is still there.

Contains Ordnance Survey data © Crown copyright and database right 2012.

Section Four

The houses and halls covered in this area are located along Durham Road, up Joicey Road across Blue Quarries then back to Carr Hill Road down to Deckham.

Aldersyde

Planning was approved on 1st December 1909 for Robert Kelly to build a villa on the east side of Durham Road on the Musgrave Estate. The villa was called Aldersyde. Robert Kelly owned the printing premises on the corner of Ellison Street West and West Street opposite Shephards, where the Interchange Centre is today. Behind the house stands a quite impressive building which would have been the stable block.

Photograph taken – February 2010.

Carr Hill House

Carr Hill House was situated on the Causeway, Carr Hill. It was a substantial three storeyed property. The gardens were laid out to lawn and trees backing onto Pottery Lane. Carr Hill was once a small village isolated from Gateshead and Wrekenton.

Mr George Johnson Kenmir and his wife lived at Carr Hill House from around 1853 for twenty years. Kenmir was a solicitor, town clerk between 1854 and 1855, clerk of the borough-holders and a freeman of Gateshead. In 1865 Kenmir purchased 12 acres of the Park Estate for £5,555, where the Chandless Estate was built between 1866 and 1869. In 1870 Mr and Mrs Kenmir were elected members of

Courtesy of Jennifer D Goddard (née Peirson).

30

the Natural History Society of Northumberland, Durham and Newcastle upon Tyne.

In 1873 Joseph Peirson of Peirson & Co merchants and general brokers of Wellington Street lived at Carr Hill House.

The image right is Joseph and Margaret Peirson in 1864.

By 1876 a Mrs Greener lived at Carr Hill House and around 1883 Mr George Geipel, a market gardener, and his wife. Mrs Geipel died on the 9th January 1886, aged 64, and was buried at Gateshead Fell.

The 1911 census shows engineer Mr W Coaker and solicitor Mr L H Booth along with Captain Upton and Roger Dawson all living at Carr Hill House. Carr Hill House also had its own lodge which was situated on Old Durham Road.

W. STONEHOUSE, PHOTO.   WHITBY

Courtesy of Jennifer D Goddard (née Peirson).

Clarendon House

Clarendon House is situated on the corner of Durham Road and Joicey Road, opposite The Chesters. The house is a substantial stone building with large bay windows on two floors and wrought iron gates leading up a pathway to the front of the house. Clarendon House is on Gateshead Council's list of notable buildings.

Photograph taken – October 2011.

Deckham Hall

Deckham Hall in 1614 belonged to Thomas Dackham and was later occupied by Henry Midford, his son-in-law. Ownership later passed to the Liddell and Milbank families until 1719 when part of the estate was purchased by William Cotesworth.

Miles Bowker was born at Deckham Hall in 1759; his father Thomas Bowker was a merchant. Miles married Anna Maria Mitford on 10th May 1800, and farmed the land at Deckham Hall.

Miles was over 60 when he left for South Africa leading a party of settlers and achieved much in the land of his adoption. There is a bust of him in the Albany Museum in Grahamstown, South Africa. (Image on page 32.)

Courtesy of Margaret Manning 2005.

Courtesy of Margaret Manning 2005 (Copyright Andrew Bowker).

Described in 1809 as 'fit for the reception of a gentleman's family', the Hall had delightful views of the country to the west, north and south and to the east the sea. The main reception hall at Deckham Hall was distinguished by its large fire place. At the front of the house was a pleasure ground and behind was a garden and orchard planted with fruit trees. The front of the Hall was in a different parish from the back as the front was in Gateshead and the back was in Heworth Chapelry.

In 1817 the Hall was sold for £7,100 to William James who substantially rebuilt the house. The estate around 1858 was sold by the James' family to Benjamin Bigger, a Newcastle merchant and Mayor of Gateshead in 1861 and 1862.

Benjamin Bigger was a subscriber to the Historical Registers of Remarkable Events, he sold the estate in 1873 after which it was occupied by various tenants until it was demolished in 1934.

Lindum House

Lindum House, situated on Durham Road, is a square, red brick building. In the centre of the roof there are two small chimney stacks which were originally connected by

ornamental metal-work, and so the house was therefore known as the 'House with a handle'. Lindum House was built for Thomas Wright who had gained planning approval on 4th September 1889. He lived here with his wife, four children and a servant.

Thomas Wright was a Railway Stores Assistant Superintendant. He was born in Lincoln in 1845 the son of a bricklayer; he married in Gateshead and lived in Cumberland Street in 1871 and Peterborough Street in 1881.

Photograph taken – 2nd February 2010.

Other residents have been Mr W Rutherford a mining engineer in 1905, and in 1911 Mr R Dunn a managing director lived at Lindum House. It later became the Constitutional Club, and is now a Social Club.

The images right show the stained glass windows depicting Sculpture and Painting situated in the porch, both original to the house. Other original features are the Merchant of Venice stained glass window situated on the staircase at the rear of the building, the tiled flooring in the entrance hall; and the ceiling rose and fire place in the room on the right hand side are still there today.

Windows in porch, photographs taken – June 2010.

Musgrave House

Musgrave House was built in 1854/55 as 'Forres Villa' for Mr J B Falconar, a brown paper manufacturer from Birmingham, and was noted for its conservatory which was located to the right hand side of the house. The 1861 census lists John B Falconar, aged 62, his wife Mary, aged 55, son Henry, aged 26, son Charles, aged 21, daughter Mary, aged 22, daughter Emily, aged 17 and two servants living at 'Forres villa', with William Lee, the gardener, and his daughter living at the lodge.

Another resident was Alfred Allhusen in 1885 whose father Christian bought Charles Attwood's chemical works in 1840 and successfully expanded the business until it occupied 197 acres on the South Shore. In 1872 Allhusens was incorporated with the Newcastle Chemical Works Company which in 1891 was taken over by United Alkali.

The house is in the Gothic style of ashlar, with tall slender chimney stacks with a variety of tall, patterned terracotta pots. The 1881 census shows John Ormston, aged 75, a shipowner, his two daughters, two sons and servants living at Musgrave; it was John Ormston who changed the house name to Musgrave. In 1886 Musgrave House was the only house on the east side of Durham Road between Belle View and Shipcote. Robert Kelly the printer lived there until 1912 and from 1913 to 1918 it was occupied by Mr J E Crofton, a bank manager. From 1919 Musgrave was purchased as a private day school, run by Alice and Florence Evelyn Elliott. The school was

Courtesy of Gateshead Council (Local History Library Collection).

later left to their nephew who sold it to a consortium of parents who ran it for a while; it was then taken over by one owner but closed in 1999.

Musgrave has been a Grade II listed building since 1st November 1982, the house and front garden are still there. In April 2005 it became residential apartments.

The image right shows Musgrave lodge.

Courtesy of Gateshead Council (Local History Library Collection).

MUSGRAVE LODGE, DURHAM ROAD, Nr LOW FELL.

Roxburgh House

Roxburgh House was situated between Sodhouse Bank and Beverley Road, the entrance to it was through an arch way next to the Queens Head Public House on Old Durham Road. Around 1893 George Charlton, a foreman, and in 1935 Mr J S Charlton were residents. The photograph left was taken in 1964 possibly just before the house was demolished; the site is now occupied by the more modern housing of Springfield Place.

Courtesy of Gateshead Council (Local History Library Collection).

Sheriff Mount North

Sheriff Mount North is a semi detached house next to Sheriff Mount South and is situated on Old Durham Road, built around 1873. In 1935 Mr J Wilson, a clerk, lived at Sheriff Mount North. The house is now split into apartments. A lodge stands on Old Durham Road next to the gateway and sweeping drive to Sheriff Mount North. The lodge can be seen on the Ordnance Survey map c1856-65 and possibly served The Old Rectory at that time.

Photograph taken – July 2011.

Sheriff Mount South

Sheriff Mount South is a semi detached house next to Sheriff Mount North, situated on Old Durham Road, and was built in 1873 for Richard Clayton, a Newcastle businessman. In the 1930s and 1940s Mr Robert Alexander Bowron, a Commission agent who had a business on High West Street, lived at Sheriff Mount South. At that time there was a croquet lawn and tennis court in the grounds. The entrance is via a sweeping drive leading up to the house next to the original greenhouse which has been converted into a bungalow. The house is now split into apartments.

Photograph taken – July 2011.

The picture left shows the decorative stonework in the wall at the front of Sheriff Mount North and South.

Photograph taken – July 2011.

Springfield House

Springfield House was the home of Alderman Sir John Maccoy, a shipping magnate. The Ordnance Survey map shows Springfield House Lodge on Durham Road at the junction with Dryden Road.

Maccoy was Mayor of Gateshead on eight occasions between 1912 and 1923. He was also the first and only Mayor of Gateshead to be knighted, and he was also admitted an Honorary Freeman of Gateshead in 1930. In 1916, in memory of his wife Rebecca who died in a motoring accident in 1914, he gave the drinking fountain that was situated in West Street, Gateshead.

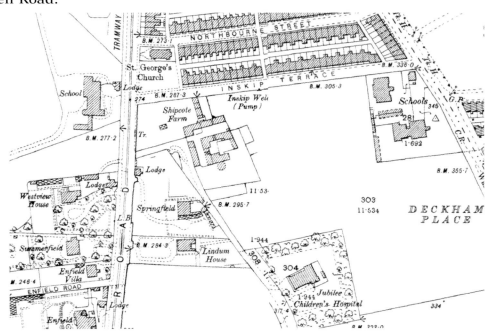

John Maccoy (right as Mayor of Gateshead) was born in Bishop Auckland, and became head engineer for Blair and Co engineers of Stockton. He had an extensive knowledge of marine engineering and was appointed superintendent engineer to the Prince Line of steamers. During a heavy storm in 1890 a steamer called Lady Ailsa was driven onto the rocks on the French coast near St. Nazaire. A salvage company from the continent tried to refloat the Lady Ailsa but without success and she was given up as lost.

Mr James Knott, one of the North East's most prominent shipping men, purchased the Lady Ailsa knowing that Maccoy was capable of rescuing the boat. Maccoy discharged 160 tons of coal and his workmen constructed a false bottom; and the Lady Ailsa was successfully refloated and towed to the Tyne.

Courtesy of Gateshead Council (Local History Library Collection).

Photograph taken in the 1980s.

The Maccoys' were known to travel by horse and trap, the stable shown left stood behind the house on Dryden Road; and was pulled down when the Springfield Hotel was extended in the 1980s. In October 2008 the Springfield Hotel closed and was demolished in 2009; today a new Springfield House has been built on the site. The residential home and Select Living accommodation opened February 2012.

The Hermitage

Courtesy of Gateshead Council (Local History Library Collection).

The Hermitage was a mansion with twenty rooms and was built in 1870 for Mr John Cotes Copland; and by 1874 it was in possession of William Clarke, an engineer and founder of Clarke Chapman's.

The 1901 census shows the Hermitage was in the possession of Mrs Isaac Tucker of Gateshead Turks Head Brewery. In 1920 it became the High Fell Working Men's Institute before the club moved to new premises on Old Durham Road. The Hermitage was demolished about 1964.

The picture right shows the imposing gateway to the driveway of the Hermitage, High Fell and was supposedly dismantled by Richard Grainger from Anderson Place in Newcastle around 1834. The entrance opened onto the old Mill Lane, which ran from Sheriff Hill to the mill at Carr Hill.

Courtesy of Gateshead Council (Local History Library Collection).

Warburton House

Warburton House was situated on Carr Hill Road; Warburton pottery is mentioned in the Newcastle and Gateshead Directory for 1795 as being on Warburton Place near Deckham Hall, near the turnpike bar, below Carr's Hill. During the 17th and 18th centuries both Carr Hill and its neighbour Sheriff Hill were described as the main areas of pottery making in Gateshead.

Courtesy of Gateshead Council (Local History Library Collection).

In 1740 John Warburton decided to base his main factory in Carr Hill. Warburton is credited with introducing white earthenware into the area and it is thought that the former Old Brown Jug public house on Carr Hill Road was named after the rich potting history of that area.

John's son Isaac carried on the pottery, and from 1811 to 1817 by Isaac's widow Ellen, when that area of the pottery which had manufactured the fashionable white ware closed. Another resident of Warburton House in 1911 was Mr H Keen, a general dealer, and Alexander Rutherford, whose daughter married John Dobson the famous architect, also lived at Warburton House.

Warburton House was demolished in 1932 and number 92 and 94 Carr Hill Road now occupy the site.

Whitefield House

Whitefield House was shown on John Bell's land survey map of 1835. The later map below shows its location off Old Durham Road, behind the Old Cannon, Sheriff Hill. Behind and to the north of Whitefield House was farm land as can be seen from the Ordnance Survey map which would have provided nice views across Saltwell and to the Ravensworth Estate. Whitefield House was demolished and Whitefield House Road is located near to where the house stood.

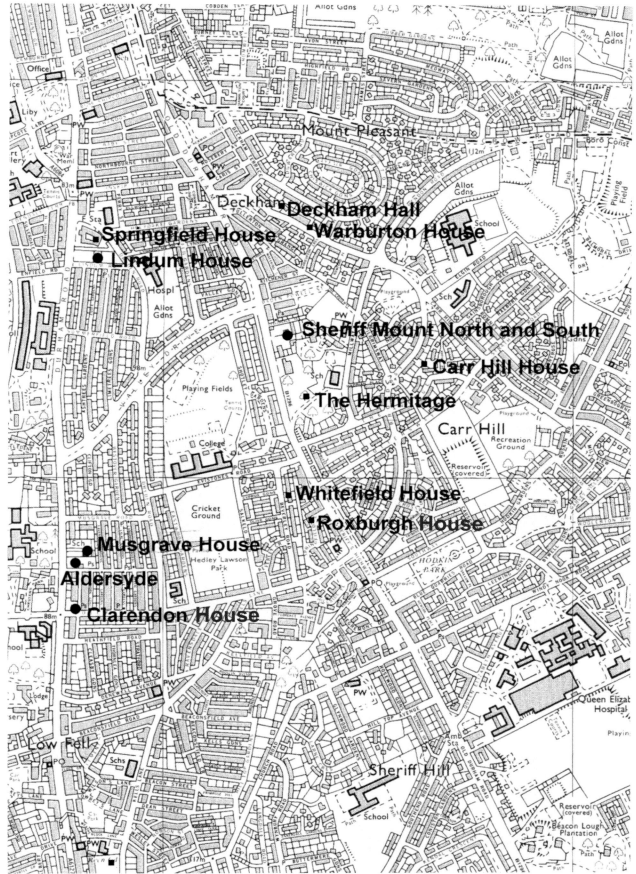

Key: Small black square ■ indicates the house is no longer there.

Large black circle ● indicates the house is still there.

Contains Ordnance Survey data © Crown copyright and database right 2012.

Section Five

The houses and halls covered in this area are located between The Drive along Durham Road, down Joicey Road and back along Saltwell Road South.

Ashfield House

The land Ashfield House is situated on, called 'Far Nancy pit field', was conveyed to Thomas Robson of Saltwellside, a gentleman, on the 1st May 1819. On 1st December 1853 the land was conveyed to William Wailes, a stained glass manufacturer, of Newcastle. Ten years later, on 3rd September, William Wailes sold the land to John Mawson, a chemist of Gateshead.

The agreement was for one single dwelling and one double villa on the land. John Mawson died around the 17th December 1867 having been blown up in an accident on the Newcastle town moor, before the conveyance was completed; so on 23rd April 1868 William Wailes conveyed the land to John's widow Elizabeth Mawson. Elizabeth Mawson was the sister of Joseph Swan who had moved to Gateshead to become a partner with John Mawson.

The garden at Ashfield was designed by John Hancock. It had been provided with a quantity of artificial rocks, which were overgrown with moss and bedded in grass and wild flowers. There were four great old ash trees which had given the place its name. It was said that Mr Mawson had planned a light railing to be placed 'on

Courtesy of Gateshead Council (Local History Library Collection).

the side of his grounds, so that every passer-by might partake of the enjoyment afforded by gazing upon the beauties of nature'.

On the 9th March 1899 Mrs Elizabeth Mawson conveyed to Lydia Jane Mawson, Elizabeth Cameron Mawson and Harriet Cameron Mawson, the land together with the mansion house and buildings erected theron called "Ashfield". The Misses Mawson had gained planning approval on the 4th March 1903 for a gate lodge for Ashfield which stands on East Park Road.

Harriett Cameron Mawson died on the 10th February 1917; Lydia Jane Mawson died on the 12th July 1924; and Elizabeth Cameron Mawson on the 9th January 1939. On the 22nd February 1940 their Executors conveyed the property to Gateshead Corporation. Ashfield House, comprising thirteen rooms, is now a children's nursery, and the land is occupied by Springs Health Club.

Bircholme

Bircholme is a large stone built house with twelve rooms and is situated at the bottom of The Drive, off Durham Road. Planning permission was approved on 3rd May 1899

for Mr John Samuel Leybourne, a coal fitter, where he lived with his wife, two daughters and three servants. In 1911 Mr W Adams, a nurseryman, lived at Bircholme and in 1937 Mr A C Nicholson, a coal exporter. In later years it belonged to Gateshead Social Services. The house was sold by Gateshead Council in 2006 and is currently privately owned.

Photograph taken – 16th February 2010.

Endsleigh

Endsleigh, which had fourteen rooms, was situated between Grove House and South Dene Tower along what was called Whinney House Lane – now East Park Road.

On the Ordance Survey map c1856-1895 there is a building on the site. On the c1895-1898 map, the house is called Team Lodge and by the c1916-20 Ordance Survey map the house is called Endsleigh.

The occupier from about 1901 was Harry Eastcott, an engineer manager, his wife

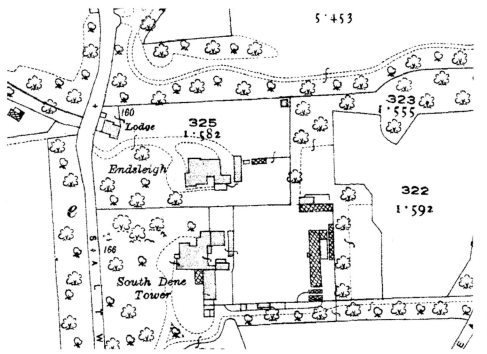

Alice, sons Harry Walker, aged 19, and Hastings Russell, aged 17. Eastcott had previously lived at 42 Bewick Road and was originally from a farming family in Devon.

Ferndene

Ferndene was situated between where West Park Road and Saltwell Road are today. It was the home of and built by Robert Stirling Newall in the early 1850s. The house was gothic in style with tall chimneys and a castellated turret at the front of the house as can be seen in the image right taken in 1910.

Newall was born and brought up in Dundee and became an engineer. He was Mayor of Gateshead in 1867 and 1868.

Courtesy of Gateshead Council (Local History Library Collection).

In 1840 Newall (pictured right) formed a partnership with Charles Liddell and Lewis Gordon and opened a factory in the Teams, Gateshead to produce wire rope using a new method patented by Newall.

As well as making cables the company started to lay underwater cables. In September 1851 they successfully laid a cable from Dover to Calais. In 1877 Newall supplied the wire rope that was used to bring Cleopatra's Needle to London from Egypt.

Newall was a keen astronomer, and commissioned Thomas Cooke to build a telescope for his private observatory at Ferndene. The 25 inch refracting telescope that resulted was the largest in the world for many years and had a tube nearly 30ft in length. Ferndene was visited by King Leopold III of the Belgians to see the telescope. After Newall's death in 1889 his son Hugh Frank Newall donated the telescope to the University Observatory in Cambridge. Hugh Frank Newall had started astronomy as a subject at Cambridge. In 1958 the telescope was donated by Cambridge University to the Observatory of Athens.

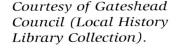

Courtesy of Gateshead Council (Local History Library Collection).

On the 1st October 1890 Mrs Newall was granted planning approval for a cottage at Ferndene. From 1906 to 1911, Ferndene was used as a Convent of Our Lady, the forerunner of La Sagesse, before moving to Newcastle. The image left shows some of the young ladies of the convent in 1911. The grounds of Ferndene were sold from 1907; the house itself remained until the late 1920s.

Courtesy of Gateshead Council (Local History Library Collection).

Grove House

Grove House is situated on East Park Road, within Saltwell Park grounds. The style of the brick work of Grove House is similar to that of Saltwell Towers. In 1858 Mr R L Burnett, a brick manufacturer, lived in Grove House which was then known as Saltwell Grove. In 1870 Mr W G Hanning, a candle manufacturer; around 1883 Mr H C Armstrong; and in 1893 Misses Ryott lived at Saltwell Grove. In 1920 Grove House and its gardens to the south were incorporated into Saltwell Park. In 1935 Alfred Lucas, a brick manufacturer, also lived at Grove House.

Photograph taken – July 2011.

Heathfield House

Heathfield is situated on Durham Road and is a two storey villa with thirteen rooms. It was built for Joseph Willis Swinburne who gained planning approval on 4th August 1856; and John Wardle was the architect. Swinburne gained further planning approval on the 7th March 1862 and in 1872 for additional work. On the 1861 census Swinburne, aged 34, lived at Heathfield with his wife Hannah, aged 28, four sons and four servants.

Courtesy of Gateshead Council (Local History Library Collection).

Joseph Willis Swinburne was a solicitor in his father's practice, who continued to run the practice after his father's death which then became Swinburne and Willis.

Swinburne was also joined in his practice, not only by his son William but at differing and later times by no less than three more of his six sons, Henry, Arthur and Charles.

Swinburne became Town Clerk of Gateshead in 1856 and held that office until his death in 1893 when his place was taken by his son William Swinburne, who held the same office until 1929.

Another resident of Heathfield House around 1879 was Theodore Lange, a merchant, who had the gardens landscaped; the most notable feature was a lake at the centre of which was a small island on which stood a glass pagoda. A large conservatory was built over a dene and elsewhere an artificial hill was surmounted by a full sized metal eagle.

Theodore Lange died on 11th January 1895, and a proposal made in 1896 to include Heathfield as an extension to Saltwell Park never came to pass. The area of the land upon which Heathfield was built extended in 1900 to approximately 9 acres. On the 12th June 1900 the trustees of Lange conveyed the property to John Thomas Lunn, a ship owner of Newcastle. In 1911 Lunn, aged 53, lived at Heathfield with his wife Eleanor Anne, aged 51, their daughter Edith Eleanor, aged 24, son Norman, aged 22, son Stanley Howard, aged 20 and one servant. John Thomas Lunn sold portions of the land and on 21st November 1925 he conveyed the remainder of the land together with Heathfield and the entrance lodges and other dwelling houses to the Heathfield Estates Ltd. On the 23rd April 1945 the Heathfield Estates Ltd conveyed Heathfield House and adjoining land to Gateshead Corporation.

Postcard – Valentine's Series.

The garden was eventually built on for Heathfield School, since demolished, and is now occupied by a housing development. The house is a Grade II listed building and was subdivided into Council-owned flats. The imposing gateway on Durham Road which was carved by Anthony Kell and John Lamb Burnie also survives although not as depicted above in this Valentine's Series postcard. The house is currently empty and the gateway is railed off. (July 2012).

Ravenshill

Ravenshill was situated at the bottom of The Drive and was built pre 1865. The house had a Pre-Raphaelite hall and an outside frieze with symbols of the four seasons on the West front. It was once the home of the artistic Sowerbys, the owners of a glass works

Courtesy of Gateshead Council.

for which Gateshead was once famous, and where fine glass was produced. John George Sowerby married Amy Margaret Hewison, daughter of a Newcastle corn merchant in 1872. A few years later with their two young children they moved to Ravenshill. The 1881 census shows John George, his wife and five children, one son and four daughters one of whom was Katherine Githa who became a notable author and playwright. The family lived at Ravenshill for a few years with quite a large number of servants including a butler. At the top of The Drive a blue plaque has been placed on the wall to note Katherine Githa.

The first glassworks established in Pipewellgate was in 1760 by Joseph Sowerby, at the west end of this street. In 1833 there were five glassworks employing about 500 men; skilled tradesmen worked an average of four days per week for £2 while labourers earned only 18/-.

During the 1850s several smaller firms sprang up, some of which survived until the turn of the century when only two companies remained, Sowerby's and Davidson's. Both manufactured moulded or pressed glass products, to give the impression of cut glass but at a lower price, and ornaments.

In 1850 Sowerby moved to East Street and by 1871 John George had taken over the firm which in 1881 became a limited company, changing its name to Sowerby's Ellison Glass Works Ltd. In 1889 a subsidiary company, Gateshead Stained Glass Company was formed, with the unusual feature that the principal employees were shareholders.

Courtesy of Gateshead Council (Local History Library Collection).

Other residents of Ravenshill have been in 1897 Mr T Emley, a senior iron manager; and from 1911 to around 1918 a Miss J E Davidson lived at Ravenshill. In 1937 Ravenshill was the Gateshead and District Trade Unions Social Club, and was eventually demolished to be replaced by a modern house for Sir John Hall of Gateshead MetroCentre and Newcastle United fame.

Saltwell Hall

Saltwell Estate was mentioned as early as 1324 and was the largest estate in Gateshead. Saltwell Hall was a substantial stone built mansion thought to date from late 16th century and much altered in the 18th century and was originally called Saltwellside Hall. In 1595 the Hall belonged to the Hedworth family, and in 1640 Sir Alexander Hall devised the manor to his brother-in-law Ralph Maddison Esq.

Saltwell Hall passed to Joseph Liddell Moorhouse who lived near Carlisle in 1770, who sold it to Joseph Dunn in 1792. Around 1805 the estate was split up by the Dunn family who retained Saltwell Hall. From 1850 Saltwell Hall was occupied by Charles Bulmer of Tyne Iron Co. The 1871 census shows his widow Ellen, aged 53, her son, her sister and family, and servants living at the Hall. From around 1879 to 1883 Thomas Hedley, of Hedley & Co, a soap and candle manufacturer, and from 1893 John Rowell, the brewer, lived at Saltwell Hall.

In 1903 much of the land was sold to form Saltwell Cemetery and the Hall, after being used as an Isolation Hospital, was demolished in November 1936.

Courtesy of Gateshead Council (Local History Library Collection).

Saltwell Towers

William Wailes, the stained glass manufacturer bought part of Saltwellside and in 1856 designed the spectacular Gothic Saltwell Towers which was built between 1860 and 1871. Saltwell Towers, originally known as Saltwell Mansion or Saltwell Park House, resembles a castle in appearance with red, yellow and black brick with towers, turrets and tall chimney stacks, surrounded by a stone belvedere.

In 1876 Wailes sold Saltwell Towers and land to Gateshead Corporation, with the arrangement that he lived in Saltwell Towers until his death, this was agreed at a rent of £140 a year.

Courtesy of Gateshead Council (Local History Library Collection).

William Wailes had originally set up as a grocer in 1830 in Mosley Street, Newcastle. However, when he was in a strong financial position he followed his first love, stained glass making, which he had studied in Munich prior to setting up his grocery business. He had visited many churches on the Continent to study the windows that he so admired. By 1840 he was in a position to set up a factory to make stained glass while his original grocery assistant took care of the grocery business. There are still many churches and cathedrals nationwide which boast beautiful William Wailes windows. One of his first windows was for Chichester Cathedral, he also designed a number of windows for churches in Newcastle and in both St Mary's and St Cuthbert's churches in Gateshead. Wailes married Jane Carr of Alnwick in 1834 and they had several children, some of whom were deaf.

Courtesy of Gateshead Council (Local History Library Collection).

Another occupant of Saltwell Towers was Joseph Shipley who lived there from 1881 until his death in 1909. Joseph Shipley was a successful Newcastle solicitor who possessed an extensive collection of paintings. His will left his art collection to Newcastle and £30,000 to build a gallery to house it. The collection was later offered to Gateshead after Newcastle had rejected the offer, and the Shipley Art Gallery was opened in 1917.

From 1914 to 1918 Saltwell Towers was a hospital, after which it stood empty until used as the local Industrial Museum between 1933 and 1969. It was forced to close due to dry rot and remained derelict and roofless for some years. The Grade II listed building re-opened to the public as Saltwell Park Visitors Centre and Café in 2004 after undergoing a 5 year restoration scheme costing more than £3 million which was part of a Heritage Lottery funded project to return the park to its former Victorian splendour.

South Dene Tower

South Dene Tower, a beautiful castellated building in red and white brick, was built by Mr W Carr around 1851. Carr sold South Dene Tower to William Wailes, who later sold it to John Marriner Redmayne in 1865 for £12,500. The 1871 census shows Redmayne lived there with his wife Jane, seven children and many servants. John Marriner

Redmayne was born in 1831 in Middlesex and with his older brother Robert Robey Redmayne were directors of Felling Chemical Co and with another Director Hugh Lee Pattinson were responsible for the erection of Christ Church in Felling.

John and Jane's son Sir Richard Augustine Studdert Redmayne became Chief Inspector of Mines and was a mining expert conducting many inquiries into mining disasters.

On the 11th October 1886, South Dene Tower and land of 8 acres was conveyed to Giles Redmayne Esquire of Brathay Hall near Ambleside in the County of Westmorland, by the mortgages of John Marriner Redmayne.

1865 – Courtesy of Gateshead Council (Local History Library Collection).

On 31st July 1890 Giles Redmayne conveyed South Dene Tower and land to Robert Coltman Clephan, a merchant of Newcastle. The house had winding staircases, alcoves, and galleries which were rather appropriate as Robert Coltman Clephan collected medieval armour, so there were plenty of odd corners in which suits of armour could stand. There was also a dene in the garden.

On 1st November 1918 Robert Coltman Clephan conveyed the property to George

Laxton Collins, a commission agent of St Mary's Villa, Birtley. In May 1922 Collins offered to sell South Dene Tower to Gateshead Corporation, but the offer of £6,000 was not sufficient. Collins resided at South Dene Tower until his death on the 13th June 1937. Collins presented the marble statue of Dionysus riding a tiger, sculptured by George Simonds, to the Shipley Art Gallery in 1926 where it can still be seen today. South Dene Tower and land was conveyed to the Gateshead Corporation by his Personal Representatives on the 1st February 1938.

During the Second World War South Dene Tower was damaged when used as an A.R.P. centre, and was later used as flats for a time before being demolished in 1956. The Crematorium and grounds now occupy the site. The building was possibly the model for Saltwell Towers.

Courtesy of Gateshead Council (Local History Library Collection).

The Chesters

The Chesters is located on the corner of Durham Road and Joicey Road. Mr Emerson Shephard, a draper, gained planning approval for a house in Joicey Lane on the 6th May 1925.

Emerson Shephard began his business in 1906 with a small shop in Swinburne Street, Gateshead, which later moved to the corner of West Street and Ellison Street in 1908. In 1908 Shephard also opened his first store in Dunston and a year later opened a store in Whitley Bay. Shephard opened further stores in Ashington, Felling, Coatsworth Road, Birtley and Hebburn between 1909 and 1924. The stores sold a variety of household goods and were very popular. The final extension was added to the headquarters in West Street and Ellison Street in

Photograph taken – April 2010.

1934 which gave the store 3 floors. On the 18th January 1946 the building was destroyed by fire and Shephards moved to Kent House on Church Street while the store was rebuilt. The new store on West Street opened in 1951, and in 1980 Shephards closed and re-opened as Shopping City. This store closed in 1986 and was later demolished; Tesco car park had recently occupied the site, which has now become part of the new Gateshead Shopping complex.

The grounds of The Chesters were sold and Chesters Park was built. The Chesters is now a residential care home.

Emerson Shephard – Courtesy of Gateshead Council (Local History Library Collection).

Ythan Villa

Ythan Villa, comprising twelve rooms, is situated on The Drive, off Durham Road. Mrs E Bone of Aberdeen was granted planning approval for a villa on the west side of

Durham Road adjacent to Bircholme on the 7th August 1901. In 1911 she lived there with her three unmarried daughters and one servant. The house is of red brick with a variety of size and shaped windows each with stone surrounds. The Lodge and a large stable block stands to the rear of the property with accommodation above. Another resident in 1937 was Mr F H Greener, a coal exporter.

Photograph taken – 2nd February 2010.

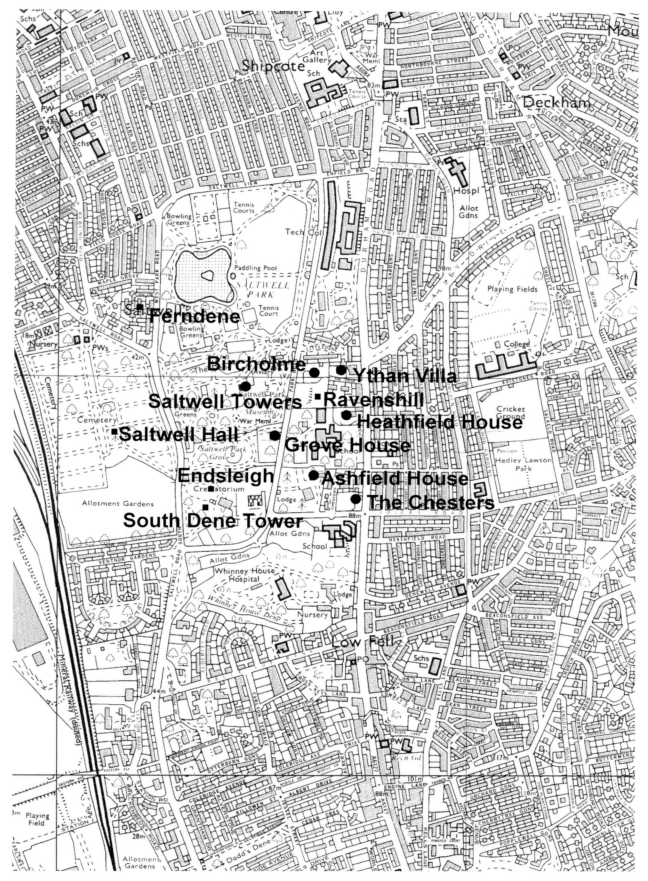

Key: Small black square ▪ indicates the house is no longer there.
       Large black circle ● indicates the house is still there.

Contains Ordnance Survey data © Crown copyright and database right 2012.

Section Six

The houses and halls covered in this area are located up Joicey Road, along Durham Road to Belle Vue Bank, and down to Derwent Crook, then back along to Joicey Road.

Appleby House

Appleby House was originally part of Orchard House and is situated on Saltwell Road South, south of Woodside House. Appleby House looks out over the Team Valley and onto the Ravensworth Estate. The house is a stone built property with sweeping drive up to the house from Saltwell Road South. A resident around 1911 was Dr Walter Galloway, his wife and daughter Theodora.

Courtesy of the owners of Appleby House.

Dartmouth Lodge

Dartmouth Lodge is situated along Derwent Crook Road, off Station Road. Mr James Norval received planning approval for three villas on 4th February 1874, one of which became Dartmouth Lodge. One resident around 1883 was Mr James Tennent, a chemical manufacturer, he was also a JP in 1897.

Another resident around 1905 for more than twenty years was Mr T Lumsden, a junior solicitor. Dartmouth Lodge is a stone built property with commanding views across the Team Valley towards Ravensworth.

Courtesy of Gateshead Council.

Denewell House

Denewell House is situated at the bottom of Denewell Avenue and Durham Road and was built around 1900.

Denewell House is a stone building of two storeys with attic rooms and was for some time a doctors' surgery; it is currently divided into apartments.

The image below is of a painting of Denewell House and Durham Road by Gordon T Kell. The painting is located in Denewell House.

Photograph taken – 2nd February 2010.

Courtesy of Denewell House residents.

Eslington Villa

Eslington Villa was originally built around the 1870s as two large semi detached Victorian Villas, North and South, on Derwent Crook Road, off Station Road. The first occupants were the Waddington family (North), an accountant with North Eastern Railway, and the Pattinson family (South) a corn merchant. In 1883 Thomas Waddington was still at Eslington North and a Mr Robert Heppell, a corn merchant, was living at Eslington South, and by 1893 Mr T Waddington, an auditor, was living at Eslington North and Mr Robert Scott Hopper, a solicitor, was living at Eslington South.

Courtesy of Eslington Villa Hotel.

The most well known family to own Eslington Villa were the Angus family from around the 1930s until 1974. Nancy Angus was a well known Low Fell character and in her later years lived there on her own. In 1974 Eslington Villa South was converted into an hotel.

At some point Eslington Villa North was changed to Roath House and more recently in 1999 the current owners merged the two properties having owned Eslington Villa South since 1987, to form the Eslington Villa Hotel.

Orchard House

Orchard House was originally a larger house which was divided into two, when the west section became Appleby House; and is situated on Saltwell Road South next to Woodside House.

The house is a stone built property with sweeping drive up to the house from Saltwell Road South. According to the 1881 census James Joicey, a coal owner aged 35, his wife Elizabeth Amy, aged 24, and son James Arthur, aged 11 months, lived at Orchard House.

Photograph taken – October 2011.

Below is an image of a tennis party at Orchard House in 1884. Back row from left to right are Miss Gordon, Mr F J Tennant, Miss Redmayne, Mr J M Redmayne, Miss Redmayne, Mr J S Redmayne, Mr Pirie, James Joicey, John Joicey and Dr Simons. Seated are Mr R N Redmayne, Miss Simons, Mrs James Tennant, Mrs J M Redmayne, Miss Joicey, Miss Gordon and seated on grass Miss K Redmayne and Mr H J Tennant.

Courtesy of owners of Appleby House.

James Joicey was born on 4th April 1846 the second son of George Joicey and Dorothy Gowland. After his seventeenth birthday he joined his late father's company Joicey and Co coal owners to work for his uncles, one of whom was Edward Joicey of Whinney House, and became head of the company after their death. He was Member of Parliament for Chester-le-Street between 1885 and 1905, and created 1st Baron Joicey, of Chester-le-Street on 13th January 1906. He held the office of Deputy Lieutenant of County Durham. He also held the office of Justice of the Peace for County Durham and Newcastle and was awarded an Honorary Degree of Doctor of Civil Law by Durham University.

Other residents of Orchard House have been around 1889 to 1898 Mr W Richardson, a coal fitter, and around 1905 to 1912 Mr W Gibson, a solicitor.

In October 2011 the present owner was renovating the house hence the gravel on the drive in the image on page 52. Orchard House is currently for sale for £1.3 million (July 2012).

Saltwell Dene East

Saltwell Dene East is situated along Saltwell Road South just south of East Park Road. Saltwell Dene East along with Saltwell Dene West were at one time part of Woodside House. The house is built of stone with a four columned porch to the front door and entered from a long drive off Saltwell Road South.

Photograph taken – October 2011.

Saltwell Dene West

Saltwell Dene West is situated along Saltwell Road South just south of East Park Road. Saltwell Dene West along with Saltwell Dene East were at one time part of Woodside House. The house is built of stone with a porch and square bay on the ground floor; and entered from a long drive off Saltwell Road South.

Photograph taken – October 2011.

The Great House

The Great House is situated on Durham Road not far from the top of Belle Vue Bank. The local historian Madeline Hope Dodds recorded that the house had at one time been an inn called The Spade and Rake, but due to competition on the Fell and Belle Vue Bank could not survive and became a private house. The house had a walled garden with a small fountain, there was also a gardeners' cottage and outbuildings which were later cleared away and became the site of the former Midland Bank.

Courtesy of Mike Scott.

At that time the house was called Fountain House. From the 1890s the house was occupied by an elderly American gentleman, Charles Forrest Cutter. After his death his widow continued to live at Fountain House and was cared for by her gardener. The owners of the house after her death found from the deeds that it had once been the Spade and Rake Inn, and changed its name to Spade-Rake. The current owners have since renamed the house The Great House.

Underfell

Underfell is situated along Derwent Crook Road, off Station Road, next to Dartmouth Lodge. Mr James Norval received planning approval for three villas on 4th February 1874, one of which became Underfell. The house is built of stone and commands a high position overlooking the Team Valley and Ravensworth. The image right shows a beautiful stone balustrade around the house.

Some residents have been around 1879 to 1884 Mrs T C Angus, in 1897 Mr John Moult; and in 1925 Mr J A Frew, a ship owner. In 2004 Underfell was placed on the Gateshead list of Buildings, Parks and Gardens of Special Local Architectural or Historical Interest.

Courtesy of Gateshead Council.

Whinney House

Whinney House is situated off Durham Road, Low Fell and was built around 1865. The house had extensive views over the Team Valley and was positioned to give expansive views of Ravensworth Castle. The Whinney House Estate was a colliery estate owned by the Atkinson and Turnbull families. The name Whinney was derived from a small coal working at the foot of the grounds known as Whinney Colliery. Henry Ellison purchased the estate in 1787 and it remained in the Ellison family for nearly eighty years. John and Edward Joicey, coal owners, purchased the land on 2nd March 1864 from Cuthbert Ellison. On 1st October 1867, John Joicey transferred his half share in the property to his brother Edward Joicey.

Courtesy of Gateshead Council (Local History Library Collection).

The garden had been designed by Albany Hancock, the famous Newcastle naturalist; John Hancock his brother, who was known as a garden designer, may have helped. The garden had two denes both of which were bridged. The bridge to the south led over Whinney House Dene to a little gate behind St Helen's Church, this was used by Edward Joicey and his family who had a private door leading into the church. The grounds also had a glazed walk leading from a large conservatory to an eccentric gazebo. The image right is the head gardener Tom Wilkinson.

Tom Wilkinson was 17 when he entered the employ of Mrs Joicey. He became one of nine gardeners working from 6am to 5pm, Monday to Friday, and 3pm, on a Saturday, for 15 shillings a week. In 1901 he became the head gardener and lived in the lodge on Durham Road.

Courtesy of Gateshead Council (Local History Library Collection).

There was a large winter garden which held a variety of blooms, extensive glass houses which held a blaze of colour and grew grapes, peaches, bananas and pineapples. The image below shows the fountain at the back of the house.

Courtesy of Gateshead Council.

Edward Joicey lived at Whinney House until his death on the 2nd September 1879. His will dated the 6th August 1879 left Whinney House to his wife Eleanor Elizabeth Joicey, who died on 15th August 1906, Whinney House was then left to her son Edward Joicey for his life.

The Trustees then let Whinney House to a Mr Fraser who was a colliery owner at Morpeth. In 1913 the house became the first Jesuit establishment in the Diocese of Hexham and Newcastle since the reformation and was renamed St Bede's Catholic Retreat, and in 1915 the house became a convalescent hospital for wounded soldiers of the First World War.

The image left shows the entrance gates and lodge of Whinney House in 1915.

Courtesy of Gateshead Council (Local History Library Collection).

In 1921 the house and grounds were purchased by Gateshead Corporation and served as a hospital, initially for tuberculosis sufferers and later for old people. In 1974 it was transferred from Gateshead Corporation to Gateshead Health Authority on reorganisation of services. The house then served as an administrative base and a centre for people with learning disabilities, and was later purchased by the Jewish Community for Torah studies.

Whinney house has been a Grade II listed building since 13th January 1983; notable features include a fine fountain which is also Grade II listed, a sunken area at the front of the house which may have been a tennis court or ice rink, stables and a lodge. On 29th May 2012, Whinney House went to auction in London at a guide price of £420,000, with planning permission to be converted into 15 apartments.

Woodside House

Woodside House is situated on Saltwell Road South, on the opposite side to the Park View Inn (formerly the Nine Pins) and is a large stone built property originally of eleven rooms. This house was built for Henry Tennant, a railway administrator, who later became the General Manager for NER. In 1854 the owner was Mr Lancelot Kirkup and by 1858 a Mr Thomas Emley. Other occupants have been in 1897 Mr Robert Norman Redmayne, a timber merchant, and Mr W Carr, a solicitor, around 1935.

The house was split into two houses and around the 1950s split into three houses, called Saltwell Dene East and Saltwell Dene West (images on page 53).

Photograph taken – October 2011.

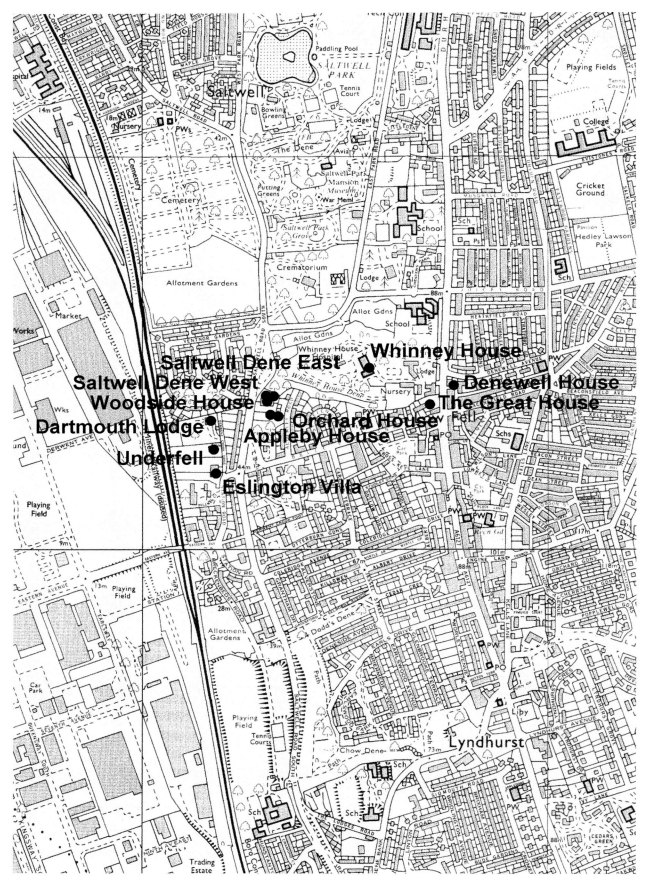

Key: Small black square ■ indicates the house is no longer there.

        Large black circle   ● indicates the house is still there.

Contains Ordnance Survey data © Crown copyright and database right 2012.

58

Section Seven

The houses and halls covered in this area are located between Saltwell Road South, up Belle Vue Bank, across to Kells Lane, then west to Station Road.

Beaconside

Beaconside is situated on Kells Lane, Low Fell and was built in 1879. It is a large three storeyed stone house with three large chimneys. The crest on the front of the building shows the initials JF. The Burgess Roll for 1883-84 shows that Joseph Forster lived here.

Joseph Forster was born 1846 and died in 1931, aged 85; and is buried at St John's, Sheriff Hill. The house became St Peter's Presbytery from around 1962.

Photograph taken – 2nd February 2010.

Belle Vue House

Belle Vue House is situated near the bottom of Belle Vue Bank and a house had been on this site since around 1822. The current Belle Vue House was built between 1865 and 1870 although the circular stone in the eave says 1877, this may have been an addition or alteration to the house. The 1871 census shows Robert Robey Redmayne, aged 42, a chemical manufacturer from Middlesex with his wife Mary, aged 34 of Coventry and their three children, Robert R jnr, aged 9, Thomas, aged 7 and Mary, aged 3. Robert R Redmayne had been one of the members of the First School Board which met 28th November 1870.

Another resident from 1880 was

Courtesy of Gateshead Council (Local History Library Collection).

59

Abel Henry Chapman. Captain Chapman (right) retired from the 19th Hussars on the 7th January 1874, after which he joined the engineering and manufacturing firm owned by William Clarke in Gateshead. A year later he became a partner with Clarke and the firm's name changed to Clarke, Chapman & Company, Ltd. By 1881 the number of workers had increased to 500 from 200 in 1874. Chapman became the Chairman of the firm in 1890 after William Clarke unexpectedly died at the age of 59; and under his direction the firm continued to grow and prosper.

Chapman was very active being treasurer of the local Church Missionary Society and also a local Councillor. In 1885, 1895 and 1899 he was Vicar's Church Warden at St Helen's Church, Low Fell. Chapman died at Belle Vue House on 24th of May 1902, aged 66, and was interred at Jesmond Old Cemetery.

At the time of his death, Clarke Chapman & Company Ltd employed over 2,000 workers and was a world leader in the manufacture of winches, cranes, boilers and other equipment. As a tribute to Chapman, the Directors,

Courtesy of Gateshead Council (Local History Library Collection).

officials and workmen erected a brass memorial tablet on the north wall of the chancel of St Helen's Church.

Other residents of Belle Vue House have been from around 1905 to 1912 Mr J M Allan, a manufacturing director, and in 1925 Mr C E Phuler, an assessor of taxes and Henry Fife Fallow (left), a house agent. Henry Fallow was a journalist for the Gateshead Observer and later became an estate agent. He was a noted local Methodist preacher and served on the Libraries' Committee from its start in 1884 becoming chairman in 1917. Fallow was also a Gateshead Councillor for 8 years and a JP for 25 years. He died at Belle Vue House and is buried at Saltwell Cemetery.

Another resident around 1937 was Mr J Petrie, a manager, and later Dr James Arthur whose surgery was within the house. In the mid fifties there was a model railway in the grounds and during the sixties the grounds were used for fund raising events.

Courtesy of Gateshead Council (Local History Library Collection).

Belle Vue House since 13th January 1983 has been a Grade II listed building. In the early 1980s it was split into a house and two flats and the land to the west sold off and two large modern houses were built.

Bracken Dene

Bracken Dene was formerly known as Alumwell House and is situated at the bottom of Belle Vue Bank along Brackendene Drive. Bracken Dene was the home of James Leathart born in 1820, the son of an Alston lead mining engineer who married Maria Hedley in 1854, the daughter of Thomas Hedley the soap manufacturer. James and Maria lived here from 1864 and had 15 children.

Leathart joined the firm Locke, Blackett and Company, a Newcastle lead manufacturing company a year after leaving school and became managing director in 1891. He was also director of the Tyne Steam Shipping Co and of William Cleland and Co Shipbuilders as well as being a Justice of the Peace for Gateshead and from the time St Helen's Church opened until his death he was People's Churchwarden.

Leathart had a fine collection of antique furniture, clocks and blue-and-white Chinese porcelain but he was best known for his collection of paintings. A great supporter of the Pre-Raphaelite movement, he commissioned pictures from several of their circle including Edward Burne-Jones. He was strongly influenced by William Bell Scott, who was the godfather to Leathart's son, William Bell Scott Leathart. Scott was a painter and artist and Leathart's painting scout. He had been master at the Newcastle school of Art of which Leathart was secretary.

James Leathart died in 1895 aged 75 and was interred in St John's churchyard. At his death he had assembled one of the finest collections of Pre-Raphaelite art and owned works by Millais, Holman Hunt, Dante Gabriel Rossetti, Ford Madox Brown, Arthur Hughes, Walter Deverell, Edward

Courtesy of Gateshead Council (Local History Library Collection).

Burne-Jones, H H Emmerson, William Bell Scott, J W Inchbold, Albert Moore, Simeon Solomon and others. In 1900 his children dedicated a stained glass window to James and Maria Leathart in St Helen's Church. The window was designed by the artist studio of Edward Burne-Jones. Another resident of Bracken Dene from around 1911 to 1925 was Mr J Fenwick, a coal owner.

Bracken Dene was later divided into three separate houses; the current owners who own the whole building are reverting them back into one property. The house has been a Grade II listed building since 26th April 1950.

Fell House

Fell House was on Lowrey's Lane, Low Fell and was built for Thomas Wilson around 1807 on the site of his parents' cottage; the name Fell was his wife's surname.

Thomas Wilson was born into a very poor family in Low Fell on 14th December 1773. Wilson worked down the pit as a trapper boy from the age of 8, and attended a school near Carter's Well in his spare time. Wilson was determined to improve his life and went on to become a school teacher. In 1798 he became a clerk of a Quayside office and later a partner in the famous Tyneside engineering firm of Losh, Wilson and Bell.

In the 1820s he began to write in dialect verse. 'The Weshin Day' in particular is well known and his 'Pitman's Pay' is another notable work. Thomas Wilson died on

9th May 1858 age 84, and was buried at St John's Church, Gateshead Fell. In 1871 a Mr Michael Shield lived at Fell House and on the 1881 census Mr William Frederick Scheele, aged 32, a wine and spirit merchant, with his wife, family and servant. In 1890 Fell House was divided into two, and houses were also built in the former garden of the house, one tenant around 1897 was Mr George Howard Patterson. Fell House was demolished in the early 1960s.

Courtesy of Gateshead Council (Local History Library Collection).

Fountains House

Fountains House is situated on Alumwell Road, and is a two storey stone building. Some residents have been Mr John Hardy in 1897, and about 1905 a Mrs Spraggon who was granted planning permission on the 6th October 1909 for a bathroom and WC on the first floor, and in 1912 Mr J W Wake, an ironmonger, was living here.

Photograph taken – May 2010.

Hillcroft North and South

Hillcroft North and Hillcroft South are two semi detached houses situated near the junction of Station Road and Saltwell Road South. One resident around 1937 was Mr C M Henzell, an oil merchant, who lived at Hillcroft North and Mr J H Smith, a fitter, who lived at Hillcroft South. Both Hillcroft North and South have been made into apartments. The lodge for Hillcroft North and South stands on Saltwell Road South opposite Coleridge Avenue. Hillcroft Lodge shown right is a brick building and has one storey at the front and two storeys at the rear.

Photograph taken – 5th February 2011.

The Dene

The Dene is situated off Alumwell Road; and is a large stone building commanding a high view across the Team Valley towards Ravensworth. The house is surrounded by a high stone wall which has two tall stone gate posts with attractive tops. Some residents have been in 1905 Mr H Taylor, a spirit merchant, and around 1911 Mr S L Smith, a manager.

Photograph taken – May 2010.

The Grove

The Grove is situated off Belle Vue Terrace, Low Fell and was built around 1840. The house is built of stone and has two storeys and attic rooms. To the right of the property is a cottage built around 1820 which at one time was connected to Grove House by a rear corridor and was possibly the servant's accommodation. The 1911 census shows Thomas Oliver a Commercial traveller aged 62, his wife Elizabeth, aged 57, and their two daughters Ethel, aged 34 and Mary, aged 22, living at The Grove. The two images below show plans from 1955 for the house and cottage to become two separate dwellings.

Photograph taken – July 2011.

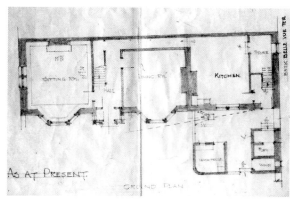

Plan of ground floor.

Plan of first floor.

Westmorland House

Westmorland House is situated off Otterburn Gardens. It was constructed in 1868 for John James Morland, a bacon factor and cheesemonger, and comprised sixteen rooms. In 1870 Morland was elected a member of the Natural History Society of Northumberland, Durham and Newcastle upon Tyne.

Courtesy of Gateshead Council.

Westmorland House, some times spelt Westmoreland, is built of stone and is a fine example of High Victorian architecture.

Other residents have been around 1893 Mr M Walton Brown, a solicitor, and from around 1897 to 1912 Benjamin Noble, a bank manager, and his wife Margaret lived at Westmorland.

At one time Westmorland was a nursing home, it is currently divided into six flats, and has kept some of its original features.

The image left shows the stained glass window by William Wailes which is situated on the landing of the central staircase.

The image below shows John James Morland's initials above the main entrance.

Photograph taken – 7th March 2011.

Photograph taken – 7th March 2011.

Wood Dalling House

Wood Dalling House is situated on Cross Keys Lane, near Durham Road, Low Fell. The house is a stone built property of two storeys with attic rooms. The 1911 census shows Robert Wilson aged 65, a blacksmith, from Wood Dalling in Norfolk lived at the house with his wife Elizabeth aged 69; daughter Kate Annie aged 35; sons Thomas Frederick aged 33, a blacksmith; and John aged 30, a draper's assistant; and daughter Mary May aged 27, a telephone clerk; another resident in 1937 was Mr F Wilson, a smith.

Photograph taken – February 2011.

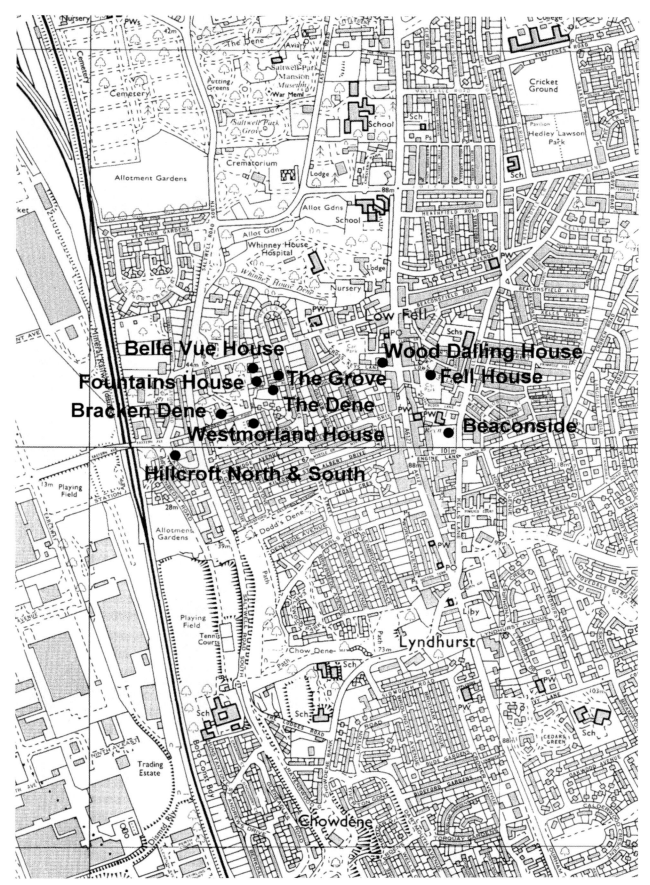

Key: Small black square   ■   indicates the house is no longer there.

          Large black circle   ●   indicates the house is still there.

Contains Ordnance Survey data © Crown copyright and database right 2012.

Section Eight

The houses and halls covered in this area are located along Kells Lane, to Beacon Lough Road and up to Old Durham Road.

Beacon Lough House

Beacon Lough House was number 677 Old Durham Road where Beacon Lough high rise flats are today. Some residents were Mr J Reay, a farmer, in 1905 and the 1911 census lists Mr Edward James Joicey, an engineer, who lived at the house for more than twenty years. He was the son of Edward Joicey of Whinney House. There were two lodges at the gate, one where the chauffeur lived, a Mr Scott who drove Mrs Joicey to St John's Church on Sunday mornings. There was also a farm on the estate and the house was at one time used as a school. The photograph shows the house roofless in 1964 before being demolished in the 1970s.

Courtesy of Gateshead Council (Local History Library Collection).

Beaconsfield

Beaconsfield was built for Richard Cail who received planning approval on 7th April 1869 for one villa. Its location was slightly south of where Melrose Avenue is today.

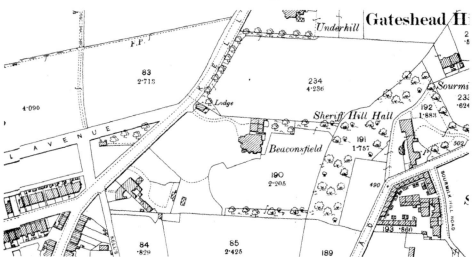

© Crown copyright and Landmark Information Group Ltd. All rights reserved 2012.

Courtesy of Gateshead Council (Local History Library Collection).

Richard Cail (pictured right) was born in Gateshead in 1812 and moved to Newcastle when he was young. Cail was the manager of a chemical works at Walker; he became a Newcastle Councillor in 1866, and was Mayor in 1871 and 1879. He was also a JP and Chairman of the Redheugh Bridge Company and a member of the Tyne Improvement Commission. He married one of Thomas Wilson's daughters; he died at Beaconsfield in 1893 and was interred at Jesmond Cemetery.

The image right
shows the Lodge for
Beaconsfield was at
the junction of
Denewell Avenue
and Kells Lane.

*Courtesy of
Gateshead Council
(Local History
Library Collection).*

Fell Cottage

Fell Cottage is situated on Kells Lane near the Dryden Road and Beaconsfield Avenue
junction. Fell Cottage was built in the mid 19th century as a substantial villa. One

occupier was Mr Joseph
Kennedy Angus around 1879 to
1893, a leather merchant.

Fell Cottage is a stone built
house of two storeys with attic
rooms. The front entrance has
fluted stone pillars supporting a
stone lintel, and the side
entrance has round stone pillars.
The Cottage at one time was
divided into two houses. The
house is currently a doctors'
surgery.

*Photograph taken – January
2011.*

Hawksbury House

In 1809 an act was passed for the
enclosure of Gateshead Fell, and a new
parish was to be formed; and one acre
was allocated for a church and
churchyard. The division of land took
a number of years, after which Sir
Robert Shafto Hawks of Messrs Hawks
and Crawshay, Gateshead Ironworks
built Hawksbury House for his son,
the Reverend William Hawks, on a site
which he called Hawksbury Hill.

St John's Church opened in 1825
and is one of the highest in England
being over 500 feet above sea level.
William Hawks became the first rector
of St John's Church. Hawksbury House
is now a residential home at the top of
Kellfield Avenue.

Photograph taken – January 2011.

Home House

Home House is on the corner of Church Road and Kells Lane and was constructed around 1858 for Edward Steel, a colliery manager, out of sandstone from the quarry which was on the corner of Kells Lane and Engine Lane, and has high stone walls around the grounds. Five stone steps lead to the main entrance and above the door is an attractive fanlight. Home House has been a Grade II listed building since 26th April 1950.

It was the home of Madeleine Hope, Ruth and Sylvia the daughters of Edwin and Emily Bryham Dodds. Emily was the youngest daughter of Elizabeth and John Mawson. Madeleine attended Gateshead High School for Girls and went to Newham College, Cambridge. She worked on the Durham Victoria History, contributing articles on Gateshead, as well as Easington and Hartlepool among others.

Courtesy of Gateshead Council (Local History Library Collection).

Madeleine and Ruth were both socialists and contributed to the monthly Gateshead News of which Ruth became editor in 1925.

Madeleine wrote 'The Pilgrimage of Grace 1536-7' and 'The Exeter Conspiracy 1538' a two volume history which she started in 1909 and published in 1915. Ruth was an author, playwright and councillor of Gateshead. She was made the first woman Honorary Freeman of Gateshead in 1965. The two sisters also undertook weekend munitions work at Elswick during the First World War.

The three sisters were active members of the Gateshead Progressive Players from their foundation in 1929 and provided much of the money for the Gateshead Little Theatre, which opened in 1943.

New Biggin Villa

New Biggin Villa is situated at the junction of Kells Lane and Beacon Lough Road. The house is a two storeyed stone building with large bay windows on both floors. The

entrance is a square stone porch and in front of the house is a nice small garden, the house faces west overlooking Chowdene towards Ravensworth.

Some residents have been around 1907 Mr J Bean, a farmer, until 1915 when Mr W R Worley, a carting contractor occupied the Villa. Mr Worley lived there for more than ten years. Mr Edward Bainbridge, the Chief Constable of Gateshead, lived at New Biggin Villa in 1954. The Villa is now a Family Dental Clinic.

Photograph taken – 4th April 2010.

Popplewell House

Popplewell House is situated along Langdale Road, near Church Road. The house gets its name from the water that poppled into a stone trough from a small well. The well

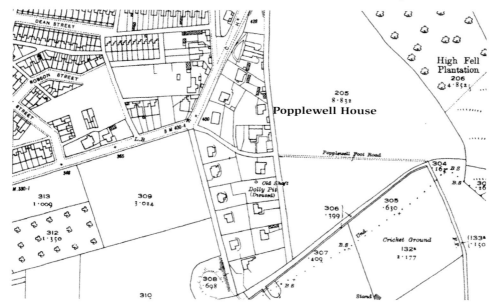

was therefore called Popplewell which was located near the Plantation, and hence the nearest house to the well was called Popplewell House.

Some residents around 1911 were Mr H G Edmundson, a grocer; and in 1935 Mr A Blackwood, a chartered accountant, lived at Popplewell.

Red House

Red House is shown on the Ordnance Survey map c1856-65 and was situated near to where Beacon Lough Road is today. It is also shown on the c1894-99, c1919-26 and

c1938-50 maps but not named on the Ordnance Survey map c1951-59. The house was near the old wagon way and to the north was the Plantation and Dolly Pit. Lorton Road is now on the site of the Red House.

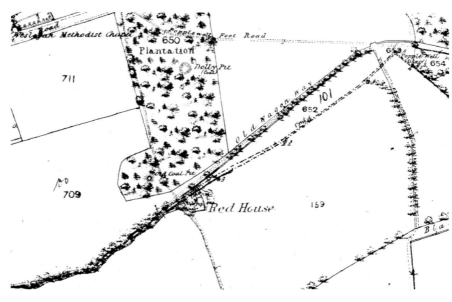

Sheriff Hill Hall

Sheriff Hill Hall was built about 1827/28 for Matthew Plummer, Rector of Heworth, after the enclosure of Gateshead Fell in 1822; the architect is believed to have been John Dobson. Matthew Plummer had acquired many allotments on Gateshead Fell. The house had two storeys built in fine ashlar with Georgian sash windows. The entrance had a fine two columned stone porch.

Matthew Plummer died in 1856. A year later the house was offered for sale and was described as a substantial dwelling in three acres of land. The ground floor had a drawing room, dining room, library and study and the upstairs had eleven bedrooms with dressing rooms. The outbuildings included a coach house, stable and offices.

Other residents around 1893 were Mr C F Lloyd, a bank manager, and in 1897 Mr John Ash, also a bank manager.

The main block of the Hall became Gateshead High School in the 1940s which it remained until 1963. The house and grounds were then acquired by a private building firm which intended to convert the house into flats. In 1964 Gateshead Council bought Sheriff Hill Hall from the developer for £6,000. In July 1967 the decision was made to demolish the Hall.

Courtesy of Gateshead Council (Local History Library Collection).

Courtesy of Gateshead Council (Local History Library Collection).

Thornleigh, number 32 Church Road, was originally the service wing of the Hall and still remains today, and has been a Grade II listed building since 13th January 1988; also some of the outbuildings are still there today as numbers 34 and 36 Church Road, these buildings are of a later date than the Hall.

The Manse

The Manse was built in 1898 on the site of the old Methodist Chapel on Church Road, Low Fell. The original building was the home of William Bell, a baker. John Wesley preached here in 1753 and a meeting room was added in 1754. The house therefore became the first Methodist Chapel in County Durham. As the congregation grew the chapel became too small and the new Wesley Memorial Church was built on Durham Road. The old chapel was pulled down and The Manse built to accommodate the Minister.

Courtesy of Gateshead Council (Local History Library Collection).

Underhill

Underhill is a large villa which appears as though three houses in one. The most notable resident was Joseph Swan.

Swan was born on 31st October 1828 at Pallion Hall in Bishopwearmouth now part of Sunderland. Swan came to Gateshead around 1845 to join his brother-in-law John Mawson, who had a chemist's shop and chemical works in Newcastle. His first wife died in 1862, and in 1869 he rented Underhill and married his wife's sister. In order to get married they had to go to Switzerland, as a sister-in-law was seen as a relation at that time, therefore it was not possible for them to marry in Great Britain.

Courtesy of Gateshead Council (Local History Library Collection).

Swan conducted most of his experiments in the large conservatory at Underhill. By 1871 he had devised a method of drying the wet plates, initiating the age of convenience in photography, for which he received the first patent in 1878.

Courtesy of Gateshead Council (Local History Library Collection).

At the Newcastle Chemical Society on 18th December 1878 Swan demonstrated his incandescent electric light bulb; in 1881 Mosley Street in Newcastle was the first street in the world to be lit using incandescent electric light while Underhill in Gateshead was the first house in the world to be lit using this method.

That same year Swan received the highest decoration in France, the Legion d'honneur when he visited an international exhibition in Paris. He was knighted in 1904, awarded the Royal Society's Hughes Medal, and made an honorary member of the Pharmaceutical Society.

The house later became a private school called Beaconsfield between 1940 and the 1970s. During air raids in the Second World War the pupils all congregated in the garage which had been reinforced. The first electric light switch ever made was proudly shown there on a plaque. Underhill has been renovated and extended and is now sheltered housing.

Courtesy of Gateshead Council (Local History Library Collection).

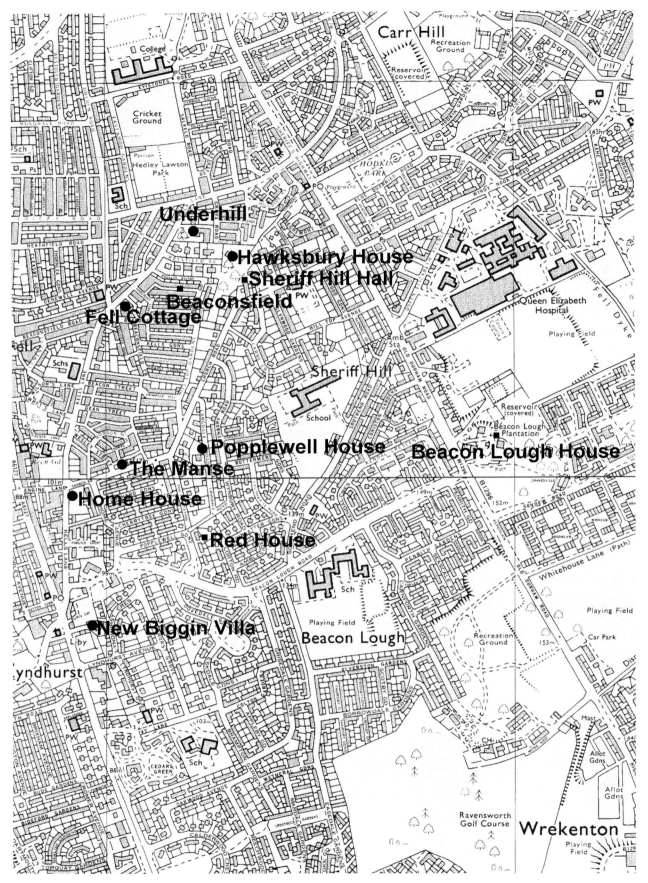

Key: Small black square ▪ indicates the house is no longer there.

   Large black circle ● indicates the house is still there.

Contains Ordnance Survey data © Crown copyright and database right 2012.

Section Nine

The houses and halls covered in this area are located from Earls Drive, across Beacon Lough to Wrekenton, then west to Chowdene.

Bleaberry House

Bleaberry House is shown on the Ordnance Survey map c1856-65, but not named on the Ordnance Survey map c1894-99. The Ravensworth Golf Course now occupies the site of Bleaberry House.

From the map shown right the house appears to have been quite small, near old walls and close to forestry land, the Dark Nursery and Mossheap Plantation. The track that passed Bleaberry House is now the road Moss Side which leads up to Old Durham Road.

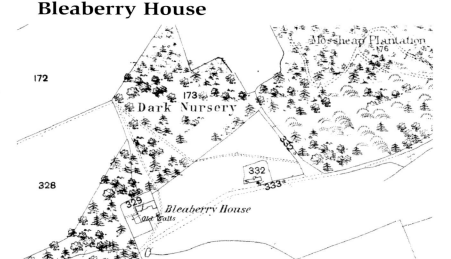

Briermede

Briermede was near the present Briermede Avenue off Earls Drive. Planning permission was approved for Joseph Grey on 1st December 1875 who lived at Briermede for more than forty years.

Joseph Grey was a timber merchant in Newcastle and a Freeman of the City and the last surviving trustee of Jesmond Parish Church. The centrepiece of the War Memorial in St Helen's Church, Low Fell depicting Our Lord and Samuel, is in memory of Joseph Grey of Briermede who died in 1918. He worshipped at St Helen's from 1876.

Gateshead Official Handbook 1950 – Courtesy of Bob Dixon.

Another resident of Briermede around 1935 was Philip Kirkup a mining engineer. Kirkup, born in 1859 in Birtley, was educated at Brampton and College of Science in Newcastle. He served an apprenticeship as mining engineer in Durham and West Yorkshire Coalfields.

He was Past President, North of England Institute of Mining and Mechanical Engineers; a Past Vice-President of the Institution of Mining Engineers; a Member of the Institution of Civil Engineers. He was also past President of North of England Branch of National Association of Colliery Managers and a JP for Durham County.

Briermede later became Briermede Receiving Home. The home had accommodation for 26 children, all of school age.

73

Cherrytree Hall

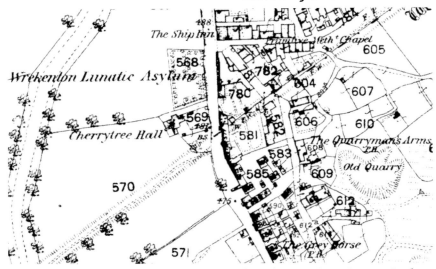

Cherrytree Hall is shown on the Ordnance Survey map c1856-65 but is not named on the Ordnance Survey map 1894-99. The Hall was situated near the present Hill Dyke along Wrekenton Row near to the Wrekenton Lunatic Asylum. The map left shows a number of buildings opposite the Hall which appears to be quite small and would have had commanding views over the valley to Ravensworth.

Chowdene Cottage

Chowdene Cottage is situated off Lodges Road. The site had originally been a farm, and appears to have been used as such until 1858 when Messers Blenkinsopp were leasing the site from Ravensworth Estate. At that time half a year's rent was £92. The house may date from around the 1860s/70s.

The house has bold square chimneys and a grand ashlar doorway, which features mock battlements with a large shield inset, and is further embellished by rope mouldings above the windows and door.

The gate piers support swirling gates dated 1953 which were erected for the Coronation. The building also enjoys a pleasant landscaped setting, with wide stone steps

Photograph taken – 5th February 2011.

leading down to a lawned area surrounded by many mature trees. There was also a lake and a tennis court to the front of the house.

The outbuildings include stables and a lodge building, but these are unfortunately in a poor state of repair. The picture left shows the exuberant ornamental lamp bracket attached to the house which is likely to be part of the original doorbell system.

The current owner has sympathetically restored the house, and planning permission is being sought to rebuild the old stone lodge.

Photograph taken – 5th February 2011.

Chowdene Hall

Chowdene (or Chowdean) Hall is shown on the Ordnance Survey maps c1856-65 to c1951-59, but not named on the Ordnance Survey map c1960-69. The Hall stood where the Stone Trough public house (formerly the Jolly Miller) stands today. One resident was Joseph Wilkin who was a member of the Royal Agricultural Society of England in 1867. The well known Low Fell farming family, the Marshalls, were the last residents.

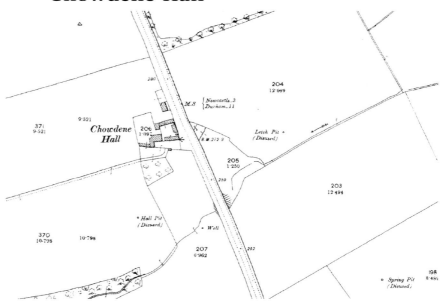

© *Crown copyright and Landmark Information Group Ltd. All rights reserved 2012.*

Craigielea

Lyndhurst and Craigielea – Courtesy of Susan Jones.

Craigielea is situated along Durham Road, Low Fell; a resident around 1883 was Mark Henderson Redhead and in 1935 William Edwin Wardill, a piano dealer.

Wardill was born at Thornton le Dale, Yorkshire, and had a piano shop on High Street West, Gateshead. He was elected a Councillor in 1895, and became an Alderman in 1909. He was Mayor of Gateshead in 1914 and 1915 and again in 1926, 1927 and 1928. He had changed political allegiance from the Liberals to the Conservatives in 1927. During his last term in office, he climbed to the top of the newly constructed Tyne Bridge, at the age of 72. In 1929 he was made an Honorary Freeman of Gateshead, and awarded the CBE. He died at his home, Craigielea in 1938 and was interred at Saltwell Cemetery Gateshead.

In the late 1930's Miss Elizabeth Twitchett, a State Registered Nurse, had returned from missionary work in Africa to care for her sick father. The family home in Prince Consort Road became a registered nursing home and in September 1939 the family moved to Lyndhurst Villa on Durham Road, Low Fell. In 1940 they purchased the adjoining property Craigielea, and the two houses became Craigielea Nursing Home where Miss Twitchett cared for convalescent patients and the elderly. When she felt she was no longer able to continue this work she donated the building to the Gateshead Dispensary Trust.

Alderman William Edwin Wardill – Courtesy of Gateshead Council (Local History Library Collection).

In 1981 the Gateshead Dispensary Nursing Home (Craigielea) Ltd was formed and in 1982 set up the Gateshead Dispensary Housing Association to build Craigielea Lodge, a care home for older people who needed residential rather than nursing care. By 1985 there were three parts to the venture, the Gateshead Dispensary Charity, the Gateshead Dispensary Nursing Home (Craigielea); and the Gateshead Dispensary Housing Association. In 2010 the three charities decided to merge in order to best serve the interests of all parties. Today the organisation consists of a single charity, The Gateshead Dispensary Nursing Home (Craigielea) Ltd known as Craigielea.

Craigielea continues to be in the forefront of care delivery to older people, continuing the legacy left by Elizabeth Twitchett. The latest development has been a four bedroom extension to the rear of the building which was completed in February 2011.

Earlswood

Earlswood was situated off Chowdene Bank near the bottom of Earls Drive in the Chow Dene. Planning permission was approved on 3rd June 1874 for Mr P Harrison and the

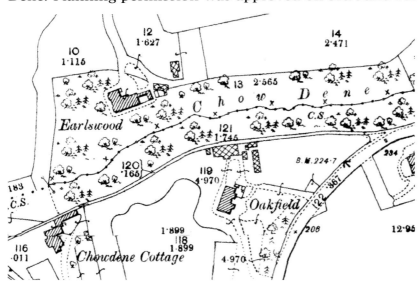

builders/architects were Swan and Wallace. Mr Harrison, an iron manager, lived at Earlswood for more than fifty years, his son Henry John Harrison was also a resident around 1897.

From the Ordnance Survey map the footprint of Earlswood appears to be larger than that of both Chowdene Cottage and Oakfield.

© Crown copyright and Landmark Information Group Ltd. All rights reserved 2012.

Glenbrooke

Glenbrooke is situated on Chowdene Bank and was built on the site of the former Sun Inn which was demolished some time between 1871 and 1881. The 1881 census shows Glenbrooke was occupied by William Barrow Tully, a ship owner, and the 1901 census shows Andrew Guthrie, a metal broker, living at Glenbrooke.

During the Second World War Glenbrooke was an auxiliary fire station and later became maisonettes.

The image right shows Glenbrooke surrounded by trees with fields in the distance over towards Ravensworth.

Courtesy of Gateshead Council (Local History Library Collection).

High Row and Chow Dene Low Fell.

In the 1960s Glenbrooke was the Meccano Boys' Club and in the 1990s it was the Cleveland Hall Boys' Club; it was later damaged by fire and sold. It is now a Residential home.

The image right is how Glenbrooke looks today.

Photograph taken – March 2010.

Greenwell House

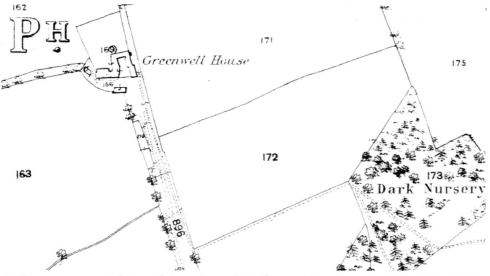

Greenwell House is shown on the Ordnance Survey maps c1856-65 until c1960-69; and was situated near Blackrow Lane, near to where Easedale Gardens and Ulverston Gardens are today. Greenwell Junior High School was built on the land of Greenwell House and Farm.

© Crown copyright and Landmark Information Group Ltd. All rights reserved 2012.

Novar House

Novar House is an eleven roomed house situated off Sidmouth Road, Chowdene. One resident was Hugh Munro a seed merchant who moved his family into Novar House around 1900 from Long Acre Farm in Birtley. His father also Hugh Munro was born in Scotland in 1829; on the 1851 Census he was living at Beamish Hall where he was the under gardener. In 1857 Hugh Munro married Ann Todd who was the cook at Beamish Hall.

Courtesy of Bob Dixon – February 2011.

According to the electoral rolls Novar House and grounds were leasehold. The house may well have got its name from the Novar estate in Ross and Cromarty, Scotland owned by the Munro family.

Hugh Munro lived at Novar House until his death in 1902. His widow, Amy, later remarried Thomas Russell Jarvie, the veterinary surgeon, who had moved to Wishaw House by 1911. In 1911 Harry Walker Eastcott, aged 29, his wife, three year old daughter and two servants lived at Novar before moving to North Dene in 1914. Harry Walker Eastcott was the son of Harry Eastcott of Endsleigh.

The image right shows the lovely stained glass window on the landing at Novar.

Novar is now called St Cuthbert's House.

Courtesy of Bob Dixon – February 2011.

Oakfield

Oakfield was situated on Chowdene Bank set in around 4 acres. Some residents have been in 1883 Mr John Young, a ship broker; the 1891 census shows Charles R Greene, an oil merchant; in 1893 Mr Joseph Kennedy Armstrong, a solicitor; in 1897 Mr William Hope Parkinson, a coal-fitter; and the 1901 census shows William H Parkinson, a steamship owner. In 1935 Ernest Hodgson Kirkup, a mining engineer, lived at Oakfield. Kirkup was a company director at Milburn House, Newcastle, and wrote an article for Transactions of the Mining Engineers Vol 83-84.

Between 1937 and 1941 Gateshead Social Welfare recommended the purchase of Oakfield as a hostel for aged people. The sketch (left) was for planning permission for the front of the house to be extended.

Oakfield later became Oakfield Nursery, and accommodated 26 children varying in ages from a few days up to five years. Oakfield was demolished and Oakfield School now occupies the site.

Courtesy of Gateshead Council (Local History Library Collection).

Ravenswood

Ravenswood is a detached stone built residence near Lodges Road, the grounds are well maintained with lawns, mature trees and shrubs. Situated on the hillside it has a beautiful south west aspect, with a commanding open view over the Team Valley, Ravensworth Woods and the adjacent countryside.

The house is approached by an entrance with gardener's lodge from Chowdene Bank.

Image from For Sale leaflet – Courtesy of Bob Dixon.

Some of the occupiers have been; around 1890 to 1893 Stephen John Humble, an accountant, around 1895 and 1897 John William Roundthwaite, an architect, between 1899 and 1915 Nicholas Henry Martin, a manufacturing chemist. Mr Martin was a well known businessman being a partner in Brady & Martin of Mosley Street, Newcastle, a wholesale and retail chemists and also opticians. He also had a chemist shop on Durham Road, Gateshead. His wife instigated the Girls Friendly Society at St Helen's Church in 1902 for young girls who had left their homes in rural areas for domestic service in towns and cities. Around 1918 to

Image from For Sale leaflet – Courtesy of Bob Dixon.

1929 Thomas and W S Lumsden, engineers, lived at Ravenswood; and from 1931 to 1939 George Raw, an engineer.

View Field

View Field was situated on Longbank in Wrekenton. Around 1905 Mr W H Price, a surgeon; and in 1935 Mr J Gordon, a surgeon, lived at View Field, Wrekenton.

Wrekenton House

Wrekenton House (see map above) was a listed building and was situated on Springwell Road; and can be seen on the Ordnance Survey map of 1856-1865. It was the largest house in Wrekenton with stables and other outbuildings with a very large walled garden. It was occupied by Dr Robert Davies and his family. Dr Davies senior was Mayor of Gateshead in 1842, he died in 1847 of typhus having contracted the illness while being in charge of a small isolation hospital erected in Eighton Banks, his funeral was held in St John's Church.

His son Dr Robert Davies jnr had two sons Robert and William Henry. Wrekenton House remained occupied by William Henry Davies's daughters who worked and supported the parish church at Eighton Banks. Jane Davies ran a society for girls at the church and wrote the only history of Wrekenton and Eighton Banks, she died around 1934. Her younger sister Mary occupied the house until her death in 1947. Wrekenton House was then purchased and occupied by Mr Lacy and his family and extensively modernised inside.

In the 1950s Gateshead Council placed a compulsory purchase order on the House, as it was required for road widening, and the house was demolished.

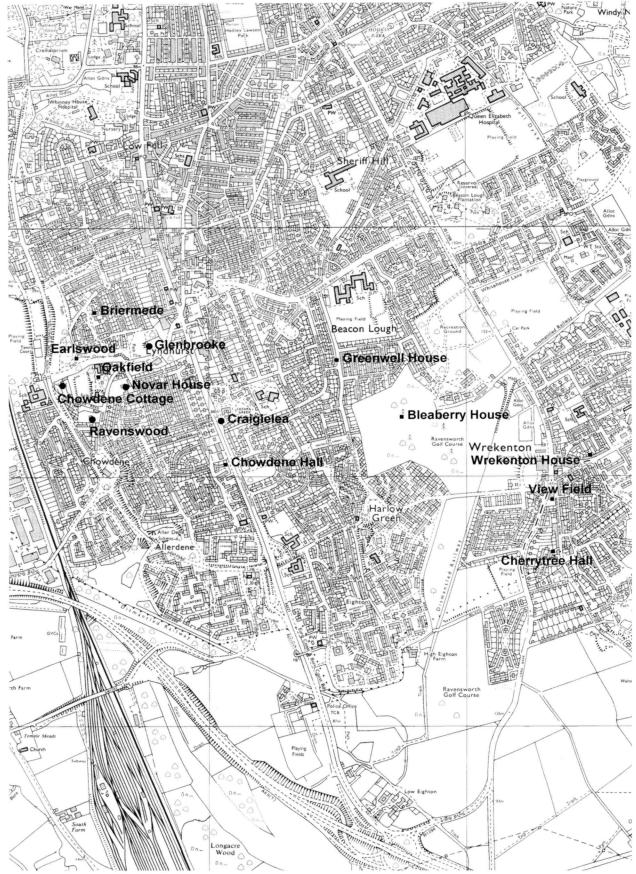

Key: Small black square ■ indicates the house is no longer there.

Large black circle ● indicates the house is still there.

Contains Ordnance Survey data © Crown copyright and database right 2012.

Section Ten

The house, hall and castle covered in this area are located on the Ravensworth Estate, beside the Team Valley.

Farnacres

Farnacres was situated south west of Gateshead in splendid isolation on the northern section of what is now the Team Valley and was originally part of the Saltwellside Estate.

Farnacres was a two storeyed long house, with a sweeping veranda which can be seen in the picture right. The house also had a museum which housed stuffed birds, rocks and minerals.

The house passed to the Liddells of Ravensworth in 1671 and by the 18th century it was the home of Nicholas Watson, their bailiff.

The 1881 census shows John Barras aged 62 living at Farnacres with his mother Isabella aged 90. His father, John Barras of Whickham had established a brewery in

Courtesy of Gateshead Council (Local History Library Collection).

Gateshead in 1770. The founder's grandson John Barras took over the company in 1884 and in 1890 the company amalgamated with four other companies. These companies J. J. and W. H. Allison of High Brewery, North Shields, W. H. Allison's Monkwearmouth Brewery, Sunderland, Carr Bros & Carr of North Shields and Swinburne & Co of Gateshead Tyne Brewery, Corporation Street, Newcastle, together with John Barras formed Newcastle Breweries.

Other tenants of Farnacres during the 19th and 20th century were Reverend R H Williamson, Mark Archer an engineer from Dunston; and Mr F W Bernard was the last occupant. On the 18th May 1936 work began on the Team Valley Trading Estate, which expanded towards the estate and the house. Farnacres was demolished in the 1960s.

Drawing room c1900 – Courtesy of Gateshead Council (Local History Library Collection).

Bedroom c1900 – Courtesy of Gateshead Council (Local History Library Collection).

Old Hall

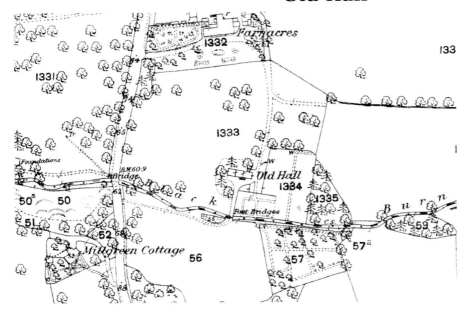

Old Hall is shown on the Ordnance Survey map c1856-65, and was located south of Farnacres; roughly where Dukesway is today, not far from Don Street, on the Team Valley, near the Western By-pass (A1). Old Hall was not named on the Ordnance Survey map c1894-99.

Ravensworth Castle

As early as 1080 Ravensworth was mentioned and by 1223 a manor house and deer park was owned by Robert de Yeland.

Ownership changed hands and by 1318 it passed to the Lumley's who remained until around 1544. A castle is first mentioned in early 15th century which was possibly a manor house with a North tower, further additions being the curtain walls, with the South tower being added later.

During the 16th century it was owned by the Gascoignes, who sold the estate to Thomas Liddell around 1607, whose son Thomas became the first Lord Ravensworth. The family changed the castle over the years, constructing a great house within the castle walls in 1724, which was demolished in 1808, only the North and South towers remained. John Nash the Royal architect who had designed Buckingham Palace created the Gothic style castle which was completed in 1865.

The castle had four storeys in ashlar sandstone and Pevsner, in his guide to the Buildings of England, said it was 'the most splendid and

c1910 – Courtesy of Gateshead Council (Local History Library Collection).

Great Hall c1921 – Courtesy of Gateshead Council (Local History Library Collection).

most picturesque monument of romantic medieval revival in the county' with an embattled and turreted exterior and an octagonal tower appearing above the trees.

The wealth of the estate was evident in its self-contained gasworks and water supply. In addition the estate employed a fleet of servants including a woodcutter and coachman, all of whom were housed on the estate. The landscaped gardens included ornamental gardens, pleasure grounds, parkland, a fountain, conservatory and walled garden.

On 28th September 1827 His Grace the Duke of Wellington stayed at Ravensworth until 4th October.

Courtesy of Gateshead Council (Local History Library Collection).

In the late 19th century the family had reached both wealth and political influence due to coal mining, but after the 5th Baron's death in 1919 this started to decline. The

family moved to Northumberland selling off much of the grand furniture, china, bronzes, manuscripts, books and many art treasures, although the estate remained in their possession until 1976.

During the 1920s it was used as a girls' school, the common room is shown in the picture left; and in 1934 and 1936 the grounds were used for a Military Tattoo.

Courtesy of Gateshead Council (Local History Library Collection).

Courtesy of Gateshead Council (Local History Library Collection).

Severe cracks started to appear due to mining directly below the house and demolition started in the 1930s by the 7th Lord Ravensworth. The stone was to be used to build a model village near the Butter Cross on the estate, but work had to stop due to the Second World War and only three houses were built. After the war the village was never completed and by the 1950s only fragments of the castle remained, the two towers and the stable block.

In the 1970s the estate was sold to the tenant. In 2003 Ravensworth Castle ruins featured on the BBC series which looked at buildings to rescue, unfortunately it was unsuccessful.

Since 18th November 1985 the remains of Ravensworth Castle have been Grade II* listed and is on English Heritage's 'buildings at risk' register.

Below are two images showing demolition in 1954.

Courtesy of Gateshead Council (Local History Library Collection).

Courtesy of Gateshead Council (Local History Library Collection).

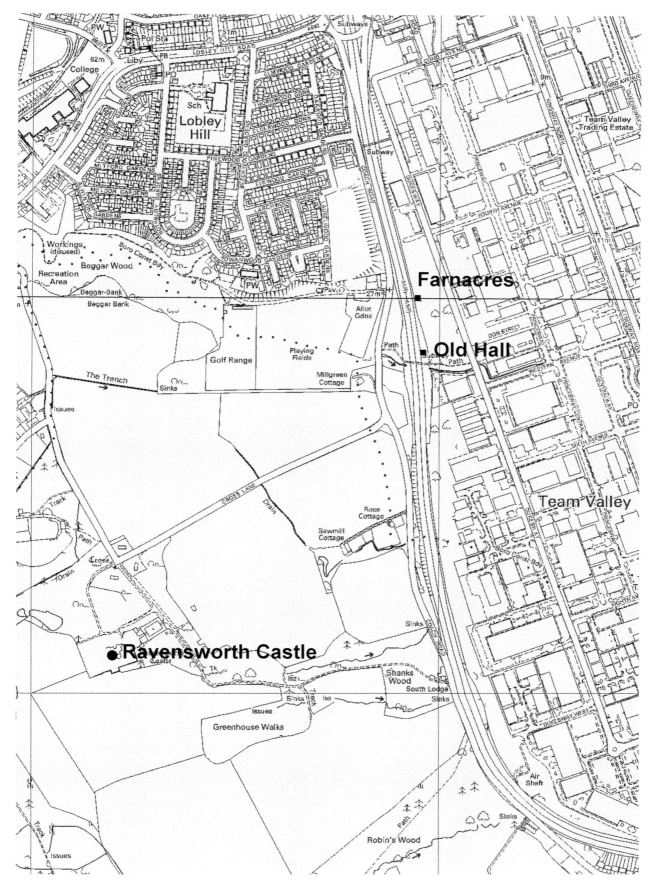

Key: Small black square ■ indicates the house is no longer there.

Large black circle ● indicates the house is still there.

Contains Ordnance Survey data © Crown copyright and database right 2012.

Index

Bibliography

Atkinson, Sid (2001) The Church on The Bank
Carlton, Ian, Clarke (1974) A Short History of Gateshead
Christies Annual Directory for Newcastle, Gateshead, Jarrow and all the adjoining Towns and Villages 1795-1935
Dodds, Madeline Hope (Unpublished 1965/66) History of Low Fell
Faulkner, Thomas Beacock, Peter and Jones, Paul (2006) Newcastle and Gateshead Architecture and Heritage
Fordyce, Thomas and Sykes, John (1847) Historical Register of Remarkable Events
Mackenzie, Eneas and Ross, Marvin (1834) An historical, topographical, and descriptive view of County Durham Volume 1
McCombie Grace (2009) Pevsner Architectural Guides Newcastle and Gateshead
Manders, F.W.D (1974) A History of Gateshead
Manders, F.W.D. (1979) Gateshead in Times Past
Meadows, Peter and Waterson, Edward (1993) Lost Houses of County Durham
Office Directory of Durham and Northumberland 1879
Pevsner Nikolaus The Buildings of England COUNTY DURHAM (2nd Ed revised by Elizabeth Williamson)
Riley, Patricia (2009) Looking for Githa
Rogers, Frank (1974) Gateshead: An Early Victorian Boom Town
Rogerson and Tuxford (January-June 1867) The Farmer's magazine Vol.XXX1

Gateshead Official Handbook 1950
The Gateshead Observer – 1st March 1845 and 26th August 1876
Lindum House – Deeds
Postcard (Gates of Heathfield House) Valentine's Series
UK census

mysite.verizon.net/cbladey/sang/bards.html July 2011
swinburne-jackson.co.uk/background.html 5 January 2011
thepeerage.com 9 January 2011
www.benshamgrove.org.uk July 2010
www.bowker.info 28 July 2010
www.british-history.ac.uk   ok 6 January 2011
www.clevelandhall.org.uk July 2010
www.craigieleacare.co.uk July 2010
www.dmm.org.uk 6 January 2011
www.en.wikipedia.org/wiki/Joseph_Swan July 2011
www.en.wikipedia.org/wiki/Wilson_Worsdell July 2010
www.eslingtonvilla.co.uk 3 October 2010
www.gateshead-history.com July 2010
www.gis.durham.gov.uk/website/interMAP/viewer.htm July 2010
www.isee.gateshead.gov.uk March 2010
www.johnolsen.org.uk/tree/n03.htm June 2010
www.localhistorygateshead.com 6 January 2011
www.pressedintime.com/sowerby.htm 5 January 2011
www.sthelenslowfell.com August 2010
www.stmaryschurchheworth.com/ August 2010
www.sunnisidelocalhistorysociety.co.uk July 2011

Gateshead Local History Society

Gateshead Local History Society was formed in September 1964 by Gateshead Libraries and the membership has continued to grow year on year.

We meet at Gateshead Library, Prince Consort Road on the first Thursday of each month from September to April (excluding January) at 7.00pm.

Our Local History nights are made up of various activities such as talks by visiting speakers, members evenings and quizzes. We also attend history fairs, undertake research activities, visit historical places of interest and go on walks of the town.

The Society is currently working in association with The BALTIC Centre for Contemporary Art on a project called 'A Story Through the Time Lens'. It is a Heritage Lottery Fund project through their Young Roots programme. The project aims to broaden young people's understanding of their culture and heritage through practical workshops and research.

Through the production of this book Gateshead Local History Society has become more involved with Community Groups and Schools in Gateshead.

New members are always welcome.

To find out more about Gateshead Local History Society visit our website

www.gatesheadlocalhistory.org.uk

or email us at gatesheadlhs@gmail.com